GUIDE TO UNDERSTANDING THE BIBLE

BY: THE MOST HONORABLE MR. ELIJAH MUHAMMAD

NWNOI Publications
PO Box 8466
Newark, NJ 07108
1-866-910-6920

www.nwnoi.org

Copyright 2025 © by Elijah Muhammad

All rights reserved. This book, or any parts thereof, may not be reproduced in any form without permission.

Library of Congress Cataloging-In-Publication Data:
Guide To Understanding The Bible

Hardcover ISBN: 978-1-957954-82-0
Paperback ISBN: 978-1-957954-87-5
E-Book ISBN: 978-1-957954-83-7
Audiobook ISBN: 978-1-957954-84-4
LCCN: 2025933891

Religion / Islam / General
Religion / Christianity / General
Religion / Comparative Religion
Religion / Biblical Studies / General
Religion / Ethics
Social Science / Black Studies (Global)
History / African American & Black Studies
Philosophy / Religious
Theology / Liberation Theology
Cultural Studies / African American Religion and Spirituality

Creative Direction & Layout by
Art Supplied Gfx
www.artdiggs.com

Printed in USA

A Tribute of Gratitude and Excellence

I extend my deepest gratitude to the **New World Nation of Islam FOI** and the following sisters for their contributions:

- **Sister AC Ukht Hadiyah Muhammad**
- **Sister Muquarabun Ali**

A special thank you to **Alah Adams** for the meticulous proofreading.

Your dedication and excellence to this great work are truly appreciated.

- Sister FSC Mutadirah Ali

*This guide is only the beginning. For those who wish to absorb these teachings more deeply, an **audiobook version of Guide to Understanding the Bible** is available. Listen anytime, anywhere, and let the wisdom unfold with you on the go.*

 www.nwnoimedia.com

Table of Contents

Reference #1: Accepted Guidance of Serpent 2
Reference #2: Against Friendship With Devils 4
Reference #3: Against Nature To Love Your Enemies 5
Reference #4: Against Workers Of Iniquity 6
Reference #5: Agreement Broken 7
Reference #6: America And Negro Symbol As Eagle And Carcass 8
Reference #7: America Compared With Babylon 8
Reference #8: America Modern Babylon 9
Reference #9: America's Scientists Troubled 10
Reference #10: Answer To Charges 12
Reference #11: Be Fruitful and Multiply 13
Reference 12: Be Not Deceived 15
Reference 13: Both Cast In Lake Of Fire 16
Reference 14: Bounds Of Their Habitations 18
Reference 40: Everlasting Life 18
Reference 82: Race Of Devils 18
Reference 86: Shall Never Hunger 19
Reference 103: Thou Shall Be Saved 20
Reference 15: Bowed To Golden Calf 34
Reference 16: Bring You Into Your Own Land 36
Reference 17: Came From East 38

Reference 18: Chastisement As Consequence Of Rejection 40

Reference 19: Chastisement As Consequence Of Rejection 40

Reference 20: Chastisement As Consequence Of Rejection 40

Reference 21: Come Out Of Her 43

Reference 22: Coming of God 44

Reference 105: Teman, A Son Of Esau 46

Reference 114: Thy People 47

Reference 122: Work Of God Against Enemy 47

Reference 23: Coming Of Son Of Man 49

Reference 24: Created Them In His Image 53

Reference 25: Creating A Race 55

Reference 26: Curse Of Noah 57

Reference 27: Dan Shall Be A Serpent 59

Reference 28: Darkness Was Open 60

Reference 29: Day Of The Lord 62

Reference 30: Day Of The Lord Is Near 63

Reference 31: Deceive Nations 64

Reference 32: Delivered Jonah 67

Reference 33: Devil Deceived People Of Paradise 68

Reference 35: Devil Kill Own Brother 68

Reference 34: Devil Deceived The Woman 70

Reference 36: Devils Seek To Slay The Negroes 73

References 37 & 38: Don't Try To Master Heaven And Earth ... 74

Reference 39: Enemy Sentenced to Death 76

Reference 41: Every Heart Shall Melt 78

Reference 42: Fall Of America 78
Reference 43: Fear God Who Has Power 83
Reference 44: Fear Of Man 83
Reference 45: Fearful And Unbelieving 84
Reference 46: Fed And Sheltered Israel In Desert 86
Reference 47: First Parents Of White Race 88
Reference 48: Flesh And Blood Cannot Enter Heaven 91
Reference 49: Garden Of Paradise 92
Reference 50: Gentiles Prepare War 94
Reference 51: God Pleads With You To Get Out Of America 95
Reference 52: God's Power 96
Reference 53: Great Deceiver 97
Reference 54: He Departed From Evil Maketh Himself A Prey 99
Reference 55 & 56: He Was Sent 103
Reference 57: Holy One From Mount Paran 105
Reference 58: I, the Lord, Thy Saviour 106
Reference 59: If God Was Your Father 107
Reference 60: In The Beginning 109
Reference 61: Innocent Earth's Blood 109
Reference 62: Jehovah Calls Moses 110
Reference 63: Knoweth No Man 112
Reference 64: Lazarus 113
Reference 65: Let Us Make Man 114
Reference 66 & 67: Loosening Of Devil 115
Reference 67 & 68: Lost Sheep (People) & Prodigal Son 117

Reference 69: Love One Another 119

Reference 70: Love The Brotherhood 119

Reference 71: Make All Things New 121

Reference 72: Moses Call Dan A Lion's Whelp 123

Reference 73: Nations Set For Showdown 124

Reference 74: Neither Is There Salvation (KKK) 125

Reference 75: No Other God 125

Reference 76: Not Know God By His Name 126

Reference 77: 144,000 Return To God 128

Reference 78: People Spiritually As Beast 129

Reference 79: Prodigal Son 132

Reference 80: Prophecy Of Lost People 132

Reference 81: Prophet Raised From Brethren 133

Reference 83: Race Of Devils 138

Reference 83 & 84: Race Of Devils 140

Reference 87: Redemption Of So-Called Negro 142

Reference 88: Religion Of Peace 144

Reference 89: Rest From Fear 147

Reference 90: Sacrifice Sons And Daughters Unto Devils 148

Reference 98: Should Not Worship Up Devils 148

Reference 91: Same In Last Judgment 149

Reference 92: Saw God As Material Being 151

Reference 93: Saw God Coming 152

Reference 94: Seek Kingdom Of Heaven 153

Reference 97: Shall Not Live By Bread Alone 153

Reference 95: Serpent As A Deceiver 155
Reference 99: Showdown Between Forces Of World And Allah 156
Reference 101: So-called Negro And His Enemy 157
Reference 100: Signs Of God's Coming 158
Reference 102: Son Of Man 162
Reference 103: Son Of Man Coming 165
Reference 104: Swine Forbidden 166
Reference 106: Ten Commandments 168
Reference 107: The Land Of Egypt 170
Reference 108: The Old Serpent Called Devil And Satan 172
Reference 109: The Throne Of Iniquity 172
Reference 110: Thee of Good and Evil 173
Reference 101: They Love Their Master 174
Reference 112: Thou Forsaken Me 176
Reference 115: To Be Destroyed 176
Reference 116: Truth Make You Free 178
Reference 117: Under Name Of Israel 179
Reference 118: Weapons No Good Against Allah 182
Reference 119: Who Is Able To Make War 182
Reference 120: Who Is Like Unto The Beast 183
Reference 121: Wicked Watches The Righteous 185
Reference 123: Worship White Man As God 186
Reference 124: Ye Have Condemned And Killed The Just 192
Reference 114: You Should Not Have Fellowship With Devils 193

GUIDE TO UNDERSTANDING THE BIBLE

BY: THE MOST HONORABLE
MR. ELIJAH MUHAMMAD

"In the name of Allah, the Beneficent, the Merciful. Praise be to Allah, the Lord of the worlds, The Beneficent, the Merciful, Master of the day of Requital. Thee do we serve and Thee do we beseech for help. Guide us on the right path, The path of those upon whom Thou hast bestowed favours, Not those upon whom wrath is brought down, nor those who go astray."

A GUIDE TO UNDERSTANDING THE BIBLE

The Bible referred to unless otherwise noted is the one commonly known as The Authorized (King James) Version.

"The misunderstanding of the Old and New Testaments by the so-called Negro preachers makes it our graveyard" (Message To The Blackman pg. 96) "The Bible (which they do not understand), I thought it best to make them understand the book which they read and believe in, since the Bible is their graveyard and they must be awakened from it." (Message To The Blackman In America, pg. 82) "The Bible means good if you can rightly understand it. My interpretation of it is given to me from the Lord of the Worlds. Yours is your own and from the enemies of the truth." (Message To The Blackman In America, pg. 88)

Reference #1: Accepted Guidance of Serpent

Genesis 3:6

And when the woman saw that the tree was good for food, and that it was pleasant to the eyes, and a tree to be desired to make one wise, she took of the fruit thereof, and did eat, and gave also unto her husband with her; and he did eat.

Both Jews and Christians are guilty of setting up rivals to Allah (God). Adam and Eve accepted the guidance of the serpent instead of that of Allah (Gen. 3:6). They made a golden calf and took it for their god and bowed down to it (Exod. 32:4). This was the work of their own hands to guide them and fight their wars. The Christians have made imaginary pictures and statues of wood, silver and gold -- calling them pictures and statues of God. They bow down to pictures and statues alleged to be of Jesus, His mother, and his disciples as though they could see and hear them. They (the Christians) claim sonship to Allah (God) and take the Son to be the equal of the Father, though they say "that they killed the Son." Today they take the weapons of war for their gods and put their trust in the work of their own hands.

Muhammad took hold of the best, the belief in one God (Allah), and was successful. Fourteen hundred years after him, we are successful, that is, we who will not set up another god with Allah. The fools who refuse to believe in Allah alone as the One God, if asked who made heaven and earth, most surely would say God and would say God the Son and the Holy Ghost. Then why do they not serve and obey Allah (God)?

It is a perfect insult to Allah (God) who made heaven and earth and makes the earth to produce everything for our service and even the sun, moon, and stars -- they serve our needs -- for us to bow down and worship anything other than Allah as a god. The Great Mahdi, Allah in person, who is in our midst today, will put a stop once and forever to the serving and worshiping of other gods besides Himself.

It is the devil's way of bringing the people (so-called Negroes) of Allah (God) in opposition to Him by teaching the people to believe and do just the thing that God forbids. Muhammad did not try making a likeness of God, nor have his followers done that. He and his followers obey the law of (the one God) Allah, while the Jews and the Christians preach it and do otherwise. We are now being brought face to face with Allah (God) for a showdown between Him and that which we have served as God besides Him. The lost and found members of the Asiatic nation are especially warned in the 112th chapter of the Holy Qur-an against the worship of any other god than Allah, for it is Allah in person who has found them among the worshipers of gods other than Allah. **Pgs. 74-75 MTBM**

Reference #2: Against Friendship With Devils

James 4:4

Ye adulterers and adulteresses, know ye not that the friendship of the world is enmity with God? Whosoever therefore will be a friend of the world is the enemy of God.

My people must know the truth, the Gods truth -- the time is at hand! They are reared and taught by the devils and they know it not; and being ignorant of the truth, they offer opposition to the God of their salvation, Who is the very author of Truth.

I am His Messenger. They do this because of the fear of the devils. They are made to believe that without the friendship of the devils they would perish.

The Bible warns them against the friendship of the devils (James 4:4). Whosoever therefore will be a friend of the world is the enemy of God. The sixth verse of the same chapter reads: Submit yourselves therefore to God. Resist the devil, and he will flee from you.

Do they dare resist the devils? No! Being without the truth of Allah and the devil, they are afraid; and that fear is the cause of their suffering and will be the cause of their destruction in hell, with the devils whom they love and fear. Preachers, who read and study to teach the Bible to your own people, get the understanding of it first before teaching it to the blind, deaf and dumb of your people lest you lead both them and yourselves to hell. Remember -- your white slave-masters are your translators and teachers of the Bible. They -- who will not give you justice under this law -- will not give you truth and justice in the World of God! Stop being a fool for false friendships of the devils, stop teaching your people to love their enemies, which is a lie the devils teach and claim that Jesus taught it. **Pg. 109 MTBM**

Reference #3: Against Nature To Love Your Enemies

<mark>Luke 6:27-29</mark>

But I say unto you which hear, Love your enemies, do good to them which hate you, Bless them that curse you, and pray for them which despitefully use you. And unto him that smiteth thee on the one cheek offer also the other; and him that taketh away thy cloke forbid not to take thy coat also.

Regardless of our sins that we have committed in following and obeying our slave-masters, Allah (God) forgives it all today, if we, the so-called Negroes, will turn to Him and our own kind. If the wicked can rejoice over the finding of his lost and strayed animal, or a piece of silver, or a son who had a desire to leave home and practice the evil habits of strangers, how much more should Allah and the nation of Islam rejoice over finding us, their people, who have been lost from them for 400 years following other than our own kind? We, being robbed so thoroughly of the knowledge of self and kind, are opposed to our own salvation in favor of our enemies, and I here quote another poison addition of the slavery teachings of the Bible: Love your enemies, bless them who curse you, pray for those who spitefully use you, him that smiteth thee on one cheek offer the other cheek, him that taketh (rob) away thy cloak, forbid not to take away thy coat also. (Luke 6:27-28-29). The slave-masters couldn't have found a better teaching for their protection against the slaves possible dissatisfaction of their master's brutal treatment.

It is against the very nature of God and man, and other life, to love their enemies. Would God ask us to do that which He,

Himself, can't do? He hates his enemies so much that He tells us that He is going to destroy them in hell fire, along with those of us who follow His enemies.

The misunderstanding of the Old and New Testaments by the so-called Negro preachers makes it our graveyard and must be resurrected therefrom. Moses didn't teach a resurrection of the dead nor did Noah, who was a prophet before Moses. The New Testament and Holy Qur-an's teaching of a resurrection of the dead can't mean the people who have died physically and returned to the earth, but rather a mental resurrection of us, the black nation, who are mentally dead to the knowledge of truth; the truth of self, God and the arch-enemy of God and His people. **Pgs. 96-97 MTBM**

Reference #4: Against Workers Of Iniquity

Psalms 94:16

"Who will rise up for me against the wicked? Who will stand for me against evildoers?"

As David said in his Psalms (37:32): "The wicked watcheth the righteous and seeketh to slay him". Also, Psalms (37:30): "The mouth of the righteous speaketh wisdom, and his tongue talketh of judgment." And in another place (Psa. 94:16): "Who will rise up for me against the workers of iniquity?" I have answered Him and said, "Here I am, take me." For the evil done against my people (the so-called Negroes) I will not keep silent until He executes judgment and defends my cause. Fear not my life, for He is well able to defend it. Know that God is a man and not a spook! **MTBM Pg. 10**

Reference #5: Agreement Broken

Isaiah 29:17-18 – *"In a very short time, will not Lebanon be turned into a fertile field and the fertile field seem like a forest? In that day the deaf will hear the words of the scroll, and out of gloom and darkness the eyes of the blind will see."*

Today, the white race, the blacks' worst enemies, has planned to make a last try to destroy the black man by pretending to be their friends and allow intermarriage.

Many Americans (especially the Southerners) don't like the idea, but will finally be persuaded by their more learned men when they see no other way of making a final stroke at the black man. It will be short-lived for the judgment will sit, and the agreement will be broken between the black and whites as it is written (Isaiah 29:17, 18).

The original black man has been without the knowledge of himself for a long time and this one (the American so-called Negroes), of all of his kind, is the dumbest to the knowledge of self, due to the way his slave-master teaches and trains him.

But this is the time of the awakening of this poor slave and no powers on earth or in the heavens above will be able to prevent it. For it is the will and work of Allah and His choice of the people.

He has chosen the so-called Negroes, but they being blinded and made deaf and dumb have not but a few chosen Allah to be their God; but they will, after they see more of His power displayed in the West -- and they will see it. It is going on now. It is a must with Allah to restore the lost sheep.

The black people are by nature the righteous. They have love and mercy in their hearts even after trying to live the life of the devils -- this is still recognized in them. When they are fully in the knowledge of self, they will do righteousness and live in peace among themselves. **Pgs. 107-108 MTBM**

Reference #6: America And Negro Symbol As Eagle And Carcass

Matthew 24:28

"Wherever there is a carcass, there the vultures will gather."

Woe, woe to America! Her day is near, and she shall be visited. Your enemies warn you that the third and final World War will be decided in your own country and not in theirs. Remember the old Bible's sayings: "Wheresoever the carcass is, there will be eagles gathered together." (Matt. 24:28). You must understand know to whom the parable is directed. **Pg. 300 MTBM**

Reference #7: America Compared With Babylon

Jeremiah 51:8

"Babylon will suddenly fall and be broken. Wail over her! Get balm for her pain; perhaps she can be healed."

I compare the fall of America with the fall of ancient Babylon. Her wickedness (sins) is the same as history shows of ancient Babylon. "Babylon is suddenly fallen and the destroyed howl for her; take balm for her pains, if so she may be healed" (Jer. 51:8). What were the sins of ancient Babylon? According to history she was rich; she was proud, and her riches increased her corruption. She had every merchandise that the nations wanted or demanded; her ships carried her merchandise to the ports of every nation.

She was a drunkard; wine and strong drinks were in her daily practice. She was filled with adultery and murder; she persecuted and killed the people of God. She killed the saints and prophets of Allah (God). Hate and filthiness, gambling, sports of every evil as you practice in America were practiced in Babylon. Only America is modern and much worse. Ancient Babylon was destroyed by her neighboring nations.

I warn you to let their destruction serve as a warning for America. These people has gone to the limit in doing evil; as God dealt with ancient people, so will He deal with the modern Babylon (America). **Pg. 273 MTBM**

Reference #8: America Modern Babylon

Ezekiel 14:13

"Son of man, if a country sins against me by being unfaithful and I stretch out my hand against it to cut off its food supply and send famine upon it and kill its people and their animals..."

As God says: "Son of Man, when the land (people) sinneth against Me by trespassing grievously, then will I stretch out Mine hand upon it, and will break the staff of bread thereof, and will send famine upon it, and will cut off man and beast from it" (Ezekiel 14:13).

We see with our own eyes -- but, the wicked Americans are too proud to confess that they see the bread of America gradually being cut off. Take a look into the southwest and Middle West, see the hand of Allah (God) at work against modern Babylon -- to break the whole staff of her bread for her evils done against His people (the so-called Negroes).

Texas and Kansas were once two of the nation's proudest states. Kansas, known for its wheat and Texas, for its cattle, cotton, corn and many other vegetables and fruits. They are today in the grip of a drought, continuous raging dust storms; their river beds lie bare, their fish stinking on the banks in dry parched mud. When the rain comes, it brings very little relief and does more damage than good. Snow comes -- it brings not joy, but death and destruction. After the snow comes more dust storms. With the rain come hail stones, very large stones. America has not seen the large hail stones; she will see hail stones the size of small blocks of ice breaking down crops, trees, the roofs of homes, killing cattle and fowl. Behind this terrific earthquake, the people -- frightened, killed, much sickness, and death will be widespread. You are getting a token of it now. On the outside a threat of an atomic war between the nations of the earth. Yet you have your eyes closed at the manifest judgement of Allah (God), going on in your midst to bring this country to naught.

Allah (God) has found His people (the so-called Negroes) and is angry with the slave-masters for the evil done by them to His people (the so-called Negroes). Allah (God) is going to repay them according to their doings. **Pgs. 273-274 MTBM**

Reference #9: America's Scientists Troubled

Ezekiel 21:15

"So that hearts may melt with fear and the fallen be many, I have stationed the sword for slaughter at all their gates. Look! It is forged to strike like lightning, it is grasped for slaughter."

We, the so-called Negroes, are the prey. Thou are the Mighty, the terrible ones, thanks to Allah, the Greatest, who is with us, to save and deliver us His people -- 20 million members of the Tribe of Shabazz -- who must have some of this earth, that they can call their own. Their God will give it to them. But woe unto you, the unjust judges, for the Son of Man shall destroy thee and give the kingdom to the slave. He is not to come. He is here! Believe it or not, I seek refuge in Him from your evil plannings.

You have been so busy trying to keep your slaves (the so-called Negroes) under your foot, sitting, watching, spying on them to prevent them from knowing the truth of this day of our salvation, that you have failed to see and learn the strength and power of your enemies.

You have boasted that you could police the world and have come pretty near doing so but have failed to the "Bear" behind the tree and the "Lion" in the thicket. The sky over you is being filled with your enemy's arms which can be seen with the naked eye.

Your scientists are troubled and at their wits' end to find time to make ready, as it is written: "I have set the point of the sword against all their gates; that their heart may faint, and their ruins be multiplied. Ah! it is made bright, it is wrapped up for the slaughter" (Ezekiel 21:15). Answer: "For the tidings; because it cometh and every heart shall melt, and all hands shall be feeble and every spirit shall faint, and all knees shall be weak as water" (Ezekiel 21:7).

The Holy Qur-an also says: And you shall see every nation kneeling down. Every nation shall be called to its book. Do you think that you want to be called to yours? Today, you shall be rewarded for what you did. This is our book that speaks against you with justice. Surely we wrote what you did (45:28, 29). **Pgs. 299-300 MTBM**

Reference #10: Answer To Charges

<mark>Luke 15:4, 6</mark>

"Suppose one of you has a hundred sheep and loses one of them. Doesn't he leave the ninety-nine in the open country and go after the lost sheep until he finds it? And when he finds it, he joyfully puts it on his shoulders . . ."

"Then he calls his friends and neighbors together and says, 'Rejoice with me; I have found my lost sheep.'"

We, the so-called American Negroes, are mentioned in the New Testament under several names and parables. I will name two, the parable of the Lost Sheep and the Prodigal Son (Luke 15:1,11); we could not be described better.

Before the coming of Allah (God), we, being blind, deaf and dumb, had mistaken the true meanings of these parables as referring to the Jews. Now, thanks to Almighty God Allah, Who came in the person of Master Fard Muhammad (who be praised forever), who has opened my blinded eyes, and unstopped my ears, loosen the knot in my tongue, and has made us to understand these Bible parables are referring to us, the so-called Negroes and our slave-masters.

The answer (Luke 15:4,6) to the charges made by the proud and unholy Pharisees against Him (God in Person) for eating with His lost-found people whom the Pharisees and their people had made sinners, can't be better. It defends Him and His people (lost and found sheep). He proved their wicked hatred for His love for His people who were lost and He (God) has found them. They (the Pharisees and their people) had more love for a lost and found animal of theirs than they did for the lost and found people of Allah (God).

Regardless of our sins that we have committed in following and obeying our slave-masters, Allah (God) forgives it all today, if we, the so-called Negroes, will turn to Him and our own kind. If the wicked can rejoice over the finding of his lost and strayed animal, or a piece of silver, or a son who had a desire to leave home and practice the evil habits of strangers, how much more should Allah and the nation of Islam rejoice over finding us, their people, who have been lost from them for 400 years following other than our own kind? **Pgs. 95-96 MTBM**

Reference #11: Be Fruitful and Multiply

Genesis 1:26
"Then God said, 'Let us make mankind in our image, in our likeness, so that they may rule over the fish in the sea and the birds in the sky, over the livestock and all the wild animals, and over all the creatures that move along the ground.'"

28: "God blessed them and said to them, 'Be fruitful and increase in number; fill the earth and subdue it. Rule over the fish in the sea and the birds in the sky and over every living creature that moves on the ground.'"

Moses taught the devils that if they would follow him and obey him, Allah would give them a place among the holy people. Most of them believed Moses, just to get out of the caves.

The Imams recognized the tremendous job Musa (Moses) had, trying to civilize the savages. These enemies of the righteous black nation of earth now had to take the place as the rulers and conquerors of the earth. The devils were given the knowledge and power to bring every living thing, regardless of its kind of life, into subjection.

And God said: Let us make man in our image, after our likeness: Let them have dominion over the fish of the sea; and over the fowl of the air; and over the cattle, and over all the earth; and over every creeping thing that creepeth upon the earth: and God said unto them: Be fruitful and multiply; and replenish the earth, and subdue it (Gen.1:26,28).

The above was all necessary if the devils were to rule as a God of the world. They must conquer, and bring into subjection, all life upon the earth -- not land life alone, but they must subdue the sea and the like therein -- master everything, until a greater master of God comes, which would mean the end of their power over the life of our earth.

We all bear witness that the scripture quoted above refers to the Caucasian race. They are the only people who answer that description and word for the past 4,000 years.

They have subdued the people and most every kind of living thing upon the earth. God has blessed them to exercise all their knowledge, and blessed them with guides (prophets) from among our own people; and, with the rain and seasons of the earth.

Today, their wealth is great upon the earth. Their sciences of worldly good have sent them, not only after the wealth of other than their own people, but even after the lives and property of their own kind. They have tired to re-people (replenish) the earth with their own kind, by skillfully killing off the black man and mixing their blood into the black woman.

But, the job is too big for them to ever conquer. The black nation, including its other three colors, brown, red and yellow, outnumber the Caucasian race, eleven to one. **Pgs. 120-121 MTBM**

Reference 12: Be Not Deceived

Deuteronomy 11:16

"Be careful, or you will be enticed to turn away and worship other gods and bow down to them."

"Take heed to yourselves that your hearts be not deceived and you turn aside, and serve other gods; worship them." (Deut. 11:26)

    The American so-called Negroes are gravely deceived by their slave masters teaching of God and the true religion of God. They do not know that they are deceived and do earnestly believe that they are taught right regardless of how evil the white race may be. Not knowing self or anyone else, they are a prey in the hands of the white race, the world's archdecievers (the real devils in person). You are made to believe that you worship the true God, but you do not! God is unknown to you in that which the white race teaches you (a mystery God).

    The great archdeceivcr, (The white race) were taught by their father, Yakub, 6,000 years ago, how to teach that God is a spirit (spook) and not a man. In the grafting of his people, (the white race), Mr. Yakub taught his people to contend with us over the reality of God by asking us of the whereabouts of that first One (God) who created the heavens and the earth, and that, Yakub said, we cannot do. Well, we all know that there was a God in the beginning that created all these things and do know that He does not exist today but we know again that from that God the person of God continued until today in His people, and today a Supreme One (God) has appeared among us with the same infinite wisdom to bring about a complete change.

    This is He whom I preach and teach you to believe and obey. The devil calls Him a Mystery God but yet claim that He begot a son by Mary. They call on you and me to take this Son of

Mary for a God, who was a man before and after His death. Yet they deny the coming of God to be a man. If Jesus were a Son of God, what about Moses and the other prophets? Were they not His Sons since they were His prophets?

The belief in a God other than man (a spirit) Allah has taught me goes back into the millions of years--long before Yakub (the father of the devils) because the knowledge of God was kept as a secret from the public. This is the first time that it has ever been revealed, and we, the poor rejected and despised people, are blessed to be the first of all the people of earth to receive this secret knowledge of God. If this people (the white race) would teach you truth which has been revealed to me, they would be hastening their own doom, for they were not created to teach us the truth but rather to teach us falsehood (just contrary to the truth). **Pgs. 8-9 MTBM**

Reference 13: Both Cast In Lake Of Fire

Revelation 19:20
"But the beast was captured, and with it the false prophet who had performed the signs on its behalf. With these signs he had deluded those who had received the mark of the beast and worshiped its image. The two of them were thrown alive into the fiery lake of burning sulfur."

"After what?" may be the question asked. The hereafter means after the destruction of the present world, its power and authority to rule. The Bible and Holy Qur-an Sharrieff are filled with readings on the hereafter which I will leave to you to read for proof. This subject wouldn't be necessary if it were not for that man of sin being permitted to rule.

Since he [they] was given ruling authority to try him [them] for 6,000 years, the world "hereafter" is used, meaning: After the present rule of the man of sin, because his [their] time is limited to 6,000 years. Some say: after the judgment, after the man when the man of sin and all who follow him were made. "Whoever of them will follow you, I will certainly fill hell with you all" (Holy Qur-an 7:18). The Bible says: "These both were cast alive into a lake of fire" (Rev. 19:20). The Man of sin and his people deceived the righteous by making them believe that he [they] also is one of the righteous. He [they] claims one father is the father of all, but that is not true.

We all look forward to a hereafter, to seeing and living under a ruler and a government of righteousness, after the destruction of unrighteousness. Even the people of the man of sin (the devils) are worried, disgusted, dissatisfied with their own world and wish to see a change to a better world; but they desire to be the ruler in that better world. The hereafter, some believe will be after the great War of Armageddon or Poly War.

A religious war between the two great religions of the earth and their believers, namely, Islam and Christianity; of course Buddhism will also be involved. The hereafter: there the righteous will make unlimited progress; peace, joy and happiness will have no end. War will be forgotten; disagreement will have no place in the hereafter. The present brotherhood of Islam is typical of the life in the hereafter, the difference is that the brotherhood in the hereafter will enjoy the spirit of gladness and happiness forever in the presence of Allah. The earth, the general atmosphere will produce such a change that the people will think it is a new earth. It will be the heaven of the righteous forever! No sickness, no hospitals, no insane asylums, no gambling, no cursing, or swearing will be seen or heard in that life. Fear, grief and sorrow will stop on this side as a proof. Everyone of us who accepts the religion of Islam and follows what God has revealed to me, will begin enjoying the above life here. **Pgs. 303-304 MTBM**

Reference 14: Bounds Of Their Habitations

Acts 16:31

"They replied, 'Believe in the Lord Jesus, and you will be saved—you and your household.'"

Reference 40: Everlasting Life

John 8:1

"But Jesus went to the Mount of Olives."

John 8:2

"At dawn he appeared again in the temple courts, where all the people gathered around him, and he sat down to teach them."

Reference 82: Race Of Devils

1 Corinthians 10:21

"You cannot drink the cup of the Lord and the cup of demons too; you cannot have a part in both the Lord's table and the table of demons."

2 Thessalonians 2:3-4

"Don't let anyone deceive you in any way, for that day will not come until the rebellion occurs and the man of lawlessness is revealed, the man doomed to destruction. He will oppose and will exalt himself over everything that is called God or is worshiped, so that he sets himself up in God's temple, proclaiming himself to be God."

2 Thessalonians 2:7-12

"For the secret power of lawlessness is already at work; but the one who now holds it back will continue to do so till he is taken out of the way. And then the lawless one will be revealed, whom the Lord Jesus will overthrow with the breath of his mouth and destroy by the splendor of his coming. The coming of the lawless one will be in accordance with how Satan works. He will use all sorts of displays of power through signs and wonders that serve the lie, and all the ways that wickedness deceives those who are perishing. They perish because they refused to love the truth and so be saved. For this reason, God sends them a powerful delusion so that they will believe the lie and so that all will be condemned who have not believed the truth but have delighted in wickedness."

John 8:44

"You belong to your father, the devil, and you want to carry out your father's desires. He was a murderer from the beginning, not holding to the truth, for there is no truth in him. When he lies, he speaks his native language, for he is a liar and the father of lies."

Reference 86: Shall Never Hunger

John 6:35

"Then Jesus declared, 'I am the bread of life. Whoever comes to me will never go hungry, and whoever believes in me will never be thirsty.'"

"The journey to understanding is not meant to be traveled alone. Our community welcomes those who seek knowledge and are ready to engage in meaningful discussions about these teachings. Join us and connect with others who are committed to the truth."

 https://nwnoicommunity.aitribes.app/ft/axkVr)

Reference 103: Thou Shall Be Saved

Acts 16:31

"They replied, 'Believe in the Lord Jesus, and you will be saved— you and your household.'"

ANSWER TO CHRISTIAN KNIGHTS OF THE KU KLUX KLAN *(Chapter from MTBM By The Honorable Mr. Elijah Muhammad)*

J.B. Stoner, the Archleader and Imperial Wizard of the Christian Knights of the Ku Klux Klan addressed a letter to a gathering of Muslims in Convention in Chicago during February 1957.

1 Thessalonians 2:14-16   St. John 8:44-48

CHRISTIAN KNIGHTS
of the
KU KLUX KLAN

Archleader, J.B. Stoner, P.O. Box 48
Imperial Wizard Atlanta, Ga.

"Infidels:

Repent of Mohammedanism or burn in hell forever, throughout eternity.

"The Lord Jesus Christ is the only begotten Son of God and He is the only One Who can save your infidelic souls and lead you into Heaven. Read the Holy Bible. St. John 6:35 -- "And Jesus said unto them, I am the bread of life. He that cometh to me shall never hunger; and he that believeth on me shall never thirst." St. John 6:47 -- "Verily, verily, I say unto you. He that believeth on me hath everlasting life" St. John 8:12 -- "Then spake Jesus again unto them, saying, I am the light of the world; he that followeth me shall not walk in darkness, but shall have the light of life." Acts 16:31 -- "And they said, Believe on the Lord Jesus Christ and thou shall be saved and thy house." Acts 4:12 -- "Neither is there salvation in any other: for there is none other name under heaven, whereby we must be saved." Therefore, Muhammad can do you no good.

"It does not surprise me to hear that Islam is growing among the Africans of America. It is easy to understand because Islam is a nigger religion. It has only been successful among Africans and mix-breeds and never among the white people never. As you probably know, Christianity was well established throughout North Africa by white people before Mohammed was born. As time went on more and more people in North Africa became mongrelized with African blood. Therefore, they were no longer able or willing to stand up and fight for Christianity when persecution came upon them from Arabia. Their faith in Christ was shallow and weak. Then came the bloody Islamic conquerors from Arabia who slaughtered white Christian leaders but spared the black people and mix-breeds. The Africans quickly forgot Christ, the true religion, and became Mohammedans. Some scholars have wondered why, but not me. I know why. Islam is a product of the colored race. Islam is a dark religion for dark people. I don't know why Africans would support Islam for any other reason except of race. There are several reasons why niggers should oppose it. One reason is that the Qur-an forbids Muslims to drink intoxicating drinks, whereas most niggers like to get drunk. It says also that thieves should have their hands cut off. How many niggers would be left with hands?

Christianity, the one and only true religion, has only been successful in white nations among white people, as recognized in the literature of the Christian Party. Christianity prevails in every white nation, even when outlawed, but does not appear to have roots in any colored nation that could withstand tribulation. Therefore on a racial group basis, it would appear that only the superior white race is capable of appreciating Christianity and that the dark inferior races prefer a heathen religion like Islam. Therefore, it is obvious that we Christians should work hard to preserve the great white race. Not only will we benefit; missionary work and be instrumental in saving the individual souls of millions of colored people in spite of their racial weakness and racial inferiority. We white Christians love the souls of all men, with all due respect to the racial differences that God Himself created. If GOD had only wanted one race, He would have created one race.

"To every place it has spread, Islam has been a blight and brought darkness. Islam's armies conquered much of Asia and Africa and even of Europe and caused darkness in every country that it entered and it decayed their civilizations that the great white race had built.

"Muslims, in their efforts to conquer the world, occupied most of Spain and even invaded ancient France. Fortunately, there was a great white Christian leader, Charles Martel. He saved Civilization and the white race by defeating the Mohammedans at the Battle of Tours in the year of our Lord 732 thus stopping the Islamic invasion of Europe. Later the Islamic Turks invaded white Christian Europe from the East. The Turks, under Suleiman the Magnificent, got as far into the heart of Europe as the gates of Vienna before they were stopped in 1529 A.D. In 1683 A.D., during the reign of Mohammed IV, they besieged Vienna again, but were soundly defeated by the great King John Sobieski in Poland, the hero of white Christiandom and perserver of civilization.

"One of the main purposes of Mohammedan invasion of white Europe was to capture white women. Only white women are beautiful. When ruling over white sections of Europe, part of the tribute required of the conquered people was the regular giving of beautiful white women to the Muslims as slaves. They didn't like their own dark women. The African race has never produced a beautiful woman so the Muslims were naturally not satisfied with their own black women. If the Africans were as good as whites, they would be happy with their own women instead of lusting for our white women. Your desire for white women is an admission of your own racial inferiority. One reason why we whites will never accept you into our white society is because a nigger's chief ambition in life is to sleep with a white woman thereby polluting her. Every time a demented white woman marries a nigger, your newspapers brag about the sin. The day will come when no nigger will be allowed to even look at a white woman or a white woman's picture. That will be a sad day for the men of your race who have no respect for their own women won't it? For your information, nigger is the Latin word for black, so why are you ashamed of it?

"Yes, Africans in America are ashamed of their own race. They regret that they are what they are. As proof, look at the nigger newspaper that advertise skin whiteners, and so-called hair straighteners. If blacks are as good as whites why aren't they proud of their black skins and the kinky wool on top of their heads? If you aren't ashamed of your race, why don't you strive to keep it pure and preserve it and its characteristics.

"You blacks have a lower opinion of your own race than we whites have. You hate, yes hate your own African race so much that you want to destroy it by mixing your blood with white blood. You want white blood pumped into your race because you think white blood is better and will improve you and make you less negroid, less African. You are trying to forget your heritage and your race by associating with your white superiors.

"If you were as good as whites and equal to us, you would not be trying to force yourselves into white society. You would be happy with the company of your fellow Africans. Or, is the odor too much for you? Since you niggers don't respect your own race and don't love your race enough to preserve it, how can you expect white people to respect it? I have more respect for an African who believes in Black Supremacy and racial purity than I do for an African who hates his own race and tries vainly to disown it. I admire the African who says that no white man is good enough to shake hands with him.

"I hope you will appreciate the fact that I am not a hypocrite like some Yankees who preach race-mixing and practice segregation. I actually express the sentiments and feelings that are in the hearts of most white people everywhere when I tell you that I believe in white supremacy and the inferiority of all dark races.

"Why should we whites let Africans infiltrate our civilization when Africans have never been able to build or maintain a civilization of their own? You Africans are afraid to do it alone. You are afraid that you would get lost without the white man to guide you and help you. Yet with your mania for mongrelization, you are trying to destroy the white race that has given you civilization on a silver platter. You are striving to kill the white goose that laid the golden egg of civilization. If you succeed, you will not be able to get more golden eggs because the white goose will be dead.

"A new independent African nation will be born in a few days on March 6th, 1957. Now known as the rich Gold Coast, it will become known as Ghana. Blacks will run it from top to bottom. Do you think they are capable of success or does their black blood doom them to their failure? The black Prime Minister graduated from Lincoln University here in America. Many of Ghana officials have studied in America. English is a common language in Ghana. If the Africans had self-respect and ability, they would go to Ghana in Africa and prove their racial ability by helping to build a great African nation. They won't go because they have no confidence in themselves.

"They know that their race is a lower form of humanity and cannot stand on its own feet. The Africans of America are afraid to be without the white man, and thus, admit their own inferiority.

"The British West Indies that lie off the coast of the United States will also become a new independent black nation soon. They speak English there. However, American's black people won't even go that short distance to help build a black nation because there won't be enough whites to control them and lead them around. The Africans of America are convinced that they would perish without the white race to help and protect them. Blacks even claim that white teachers are superior to black teachers. Inferiors always demand the right to associate with their superiors. When the black man cries against segregation, he is actually singing praises to the white race.

They never intended for America to fall into the possession of a dark race. Many of the founders of this nation owned blacks as slaves, such as Washington, Jefferson, and the great Patrick Henry who said: "Give me liberty or give me death."

America is a white Christian nation and no infedelic religion such as Islam, has a right to exist under the American sun. Your Islam, your Mohammedanism is not a white religion. Mohammedanism is a nigger religion. The white race will never accept it, so take it back to Africa with you. It is like the Holy Bible says about GOD'S plan for the nations of men in Acts 16:31 -- "And hath determined the times before appointed, and the bounds of their habitation." Therefore you have no place in America with your African race or your Islamic African religion.

"The Christian Party becomes stronger every day. When we are elected to power we will legally drive you out. Remember 1492 A.D. when those two great white Christian monarchs, King Ferdinand and Queen Isabella, expelled the Muslims from Spain. The Christian Party will be even more ruthless. We will not tolerate your infidelic Christ-hating religion on American soil. We will drive Islam into the ocean. America isn't big enough for the Christian Party and Black Islam, so Islam must go.

"You Muslims should be ashamed of yourselves for trying to lead the poor darkies of America into your Mohammedam hell. If they are smart, they will shun Mohammed and follow the Lord Jesus Christ, the Son of God, into Heaven and a happy and everlasting life.

Repent and confess the Lord Jesus Christ or you will burn in hell forever, you infidels. Your false religion is an insult to the true living GOD.

"May God have mercy upon your heathen souls.

"With many wishes for the failure of Islam in America, I am, Yours for Christ, Country and Race, (signed)

J.B. Stoner
Archleader of the Christian Party
P.O. Box 48
Atlanta, Georgia

My answer to Mr. J.B. Stoner and his Christian Knights of the Ku Klux Klan is as follows:

Sir:

The only so-called Negroes who love you (the whites) and desire you are those who are ignorant of the knowledge of you (this you do not know). And as soon as they awaken, as they will, to the knowledge of you being the real devils (their open enemies), they too will not shake your hands, nor want to look at you or even your shadow. The Truth of you will make all black mankind hate you, regardless of their color -- black, brown, yellow or red. This Truth of you is part of that secret that was withheld by Allah, to allow you to live your Time (6000 years). (I admit that the so-called Negroes are not only ignorant of self and you but they are actually mentally dead). Your time is up and you are now being revealed, and you will by no means be able to hide yourself or deceive my people any longer.

Who is to blame for this mixing -- black Africans or the white European devils? Did the black Africans go seeking your white women in Europe or did you carry her to them in Africa? Isn't it true that black Africans are today asking your kind to leave them and their country, and that you won't leave without war? (They will one day throw you out!)

"How did the so-called Negroes get into America? Did they come here of their own desire for America and for your women, or did YOU go after them in their country and bring them here against their will?"

"Did your Negro slaves every try making sexual love with their slave-masters' wives and daughters while you held and still hold complete power over them? Which of your houses and families show that the black and white males have been, and are still visiting -- yours or the Negroes? We see you day and night after the so-called Negro women whistling and winking your eyes and blowing your car horns at them; making advances to every Negro woman that walks, rides, flies or works for you in your homes, offices and factories. Not in America alone but all over the earth wherever you go among the black, brown, yellow and red people, we see that you are after our women, whom you say to be "ugly." If your women are so beautiful why then do our "ugly" women attract you and your kind? You and your kind, according to history, have been after our women ever since being on our planet. We drove you out of Asia six thousand years ago, to keep you away from our women and from mixing your wicked blood in ours. We veiled and locked our women in, to keep your adulterous blue eyes from feasting on her beauty. And the only solution to this mixture of your devil blood in our homes is that Allah remove you completely off our Planet, also those of our own who love and desire mixing with you! This is the Resurrection and Separation of us all; little do you and the so-called Negroes know or believe it!

"I have been risen to raise my people here, and to help them into knowledge of self and their God Allah (who is in Person among them) and you their open enemies (the devils). Therefore, the so-called Negroes are your own product as far as teachings and training are concerned. If you have taught them (my people the so-called Negroes) the TRUTH why are you so afraid of them believing that which you didn't teach them?

"You said in your letter, "The Muslims should be ashamed of themselves for trying to lead the poor darkies of America into your Mohammedan hell." Have you the Christian Party, led the so-called Negroes into heaven? Wasn't John Hawkins (the slave trader) a member of your Christian Party (race)? He didn't sit them (the so-called Negroes) in heaven.

"The Muslims make the so-called Negroes who believe in Allah and his religion, Islam, equal in the brotherhood of our Nation. Have you done or are you doing it now: making the Christian believing Negroes your equal brothers? You say, "Confess the Lord Jesus Christ or you will burn in hell forever." That hell must not be so hot, that one can burn in it forever and never burn up.

"Isn't it true that your Christian Party lynches and burns your black Christian believers there in your own state (Georgia)? Have you ever seen or heard of us Muslims lynching and burning Negroes who believe or don't believe in Islam?

"You said we are Christ-hating'. You have used the name of Jesus for a bait to deceive the Negroes, while at the same time you are not a doer of the teachings of Jesus, nor of the Prophets before Jesus.

"Your Bible teaches against the doing of evil. It also warns you to do unto others as you would have done unto yourself, and to love thy brother as thyself. Not any of these teachings have you or your kind ever practiced. You do not care enough for a Negro Christian believer to call him your brother Christian. And you do not think of doing unto him as you would have done unto yourself. You beat and kill them (Negro Christian believers) day and night and bomb their churches, where in reality they worship YOU, not Jesus. You even burn your own Christian Sign (the Cross) when you plan to kill or burn your poor black Christian slaves.

"You acknowledge in your letter that >Islam was the Negroes' religion,' and that Christianity was a white peoples' religion.' Then why don't you leave the Negroes alone or help them get back to their OWN religion (Islam)? And why do you insult men and the whole Nation of Islam and threaten to drive us into the ocean for teaching the Negroes their own religion, since YOU won't dare teach it to them? You further say that America is a white Christian nation, that it was founded by 'white men for white men' and that they (the founders) never intended for America to fall into the possession of a dark race. Just why then are you hindering the Negroes from going back to their OWN religion and people, especially since YOU are not going to divide this country with them and not going to treat them as your equal?

"Your Bible teaches that the Day' will come when every man will turn and go to his own. Did YOU originally own this part of our Planet? Aren't the red Indians the original owners, who are brothers of the dark Nation (of Islam) there is no part of our Planet that was ever given to the white race. The Planet belongs to US -- the Nation of Islam! And I am afraid that you might fall backwards into a lake of fire when you attempt to drive Islam into the ocean. If the ocean is ours, so is the land that you claim to be yours. Your Bible teaches you that it belongs to us. You shall soon come to know.

You accuse the so-called Negroes, who are really members of the Holy Tribe of Shabazz, of being drunkards and thieves, and suggest that they should oppose Islam because it forbids Muslims to drink intoxicating drinks whereas most so-called Negroes (or as you said niggers) like to get drunk. Who makes the intoxicating drinks? Do YOU make it or do the so-called Negroes make it? And doesn't your Government legalize the sale of intoxicating drinks? Since you say that you are Christians and followers of Jesus, did Jesus teach and legalize the sale and drinking of strong drinks? And did you find that my people were thieves and drunkards in their Native Land four hundred years ago when they were kidnapped by John Hawkins and brought over here into slavery? And haven't YOU been their master and teacher ever since? The whatever they are today, YOU (the Christian race) made them that.

"You admit that Islam doesn't allow such evils but still you call Islam "infidelic'. The Christian religion permits every evil practice that is known to mankind and legalizes them. Such religion and people you call to be of Jesus!

"We know who YOU are, and who the so-called Negroes really are. The God of the Universe and the Right Religion are not asking you, nor thank you, for trying to tell us or our people (whom you call niggers) anything of God and His religion. When we get through opening the Negroes' eyes, you will take your hats off to them.

"Your letter is headed with 1 Thessalonians 3:14-16 and St. John 8:44-48. Why not 2 Thessalonians 2:3, 4, 7-12; also 1 Corinthians 10:21. All these as well as St. John 8:44 refer to you and your race as the real devils, who even killed Jesus and the Prophets before Him, and who persecute us who believe and preach go to hell with you for believing and following you and your own Bible to pick that which condemns your own self! I am real happy to have received such open confessions of your evil self, as I am doing all I can to make the Negroes see that you and your religion are their open enemies, and to prove to them that they will never be anything but your slaves and finally go to hell with you for believing and following you and your kind.

"I hope the world of black mankind will read your letter to me. For you have many of them fooled. Some Arab Muslims think that you (the whites) can be made Muslims, but not me unless you are really born again. And it is too late for a rebirth.

"I say all so-called Negroes should give up the white race's religion and come into their own (Nation of Islam). In Islam alone they will enjoy brotherly love, peace of mind and contentment.

I will admit the so-called Negroes educated and trained by you and your kind will never be able to maintain self-rule. But they are now reaching out for Allah and Islam, and for training from others of their OWN Nation who are and have been independent long before you were even created. We all know that you hold back the very key of knowledge that would make the so-called Negroes, that you school, from ever being capable of self-government. But they will get it in Islam. And when they have finished their courses, they won't even think of building a government on your basis. The world that you have built is nothing compared to that which Allah will build with your slaves (the so-called Negroes).

"You make it clear why you doubt Ghana's success in maintaining independence; because Ghana's Prime Minister graduated from one of your schools (Lincoln University) and because its your language (English) that is the common language in Ghana. But now they are studying their own, (Arabic), language, and soon they will return to their own religion (Islam).

"You said that if the Africans of America had self-respect and ability they would go to Ghana and help build a great African Nation. But not with your schooling! If you would stop interfering with those who are trying to qualify themselves for a return to their Native people and country, within a few years they all would leave you and your evil doings. But nay! You don't want them to leave your country. No! Not any more than Pharaoh wanted to see his slaves leave Egypt. But Allah is going to take yours as He took Pharaoh's slaves, believe it or not.

"You like to make fun of your slaves whom YOU have taught and trained. But they ARE your product.

"You make the so-called Negroes do for you everything that a real citizen does and yet you will not give them equal rights as a citizen. You make them fight to keep you free to rule them and their kind.

"They (so-called Negroes) pay equal taxes, but are paid the lowest wages. Even in your own state (Georgia) they aren't allowed to use your highway filling station's rest-rooms (but will be arrested if they are seen relieving themselves in public). They are not allowed to eat in your public eating places, though they may purchase the food and eat it on the outside. Yet when your country's future is at stake you tell them that this is their country and that they are citizens of it! You know that they are fools for believing what you say knowing that you have told them the same old false story many times and many of them believe you. But not me, or my followers.

"If there was any good in you (which there isn't) you would exempt all the so-called Negroes from paying taxes, since they are your free slaves. You don't intend to divide your 48 states with them, not even one state, nor the spoils of war that they so willingly help gain for you.

"The so-called Negroes do not demand anything from you, except that you stop killing them unjustly and give them equal justice under your laws as you do for yourself, and equal WAGES as you do for your kind and for the same labor. No, not land for themselves, nor instruments and money to go elsewhere which you have acquired from their labor, sweat and blood. No real civilized people would be asking for such small pay in return for four hundred years of free labor, free blood, life and for the use (misuse) of their women by you at your will -- only a foolish people without knowledge of you and their own kind would accept that.

"Thanks, thanks to Allah, our God, in the Person of Master Fard Muhammad, the Great Mahdi, who was to come and has come, to restore -- Awe", who were lost from our Own -- the Kingdom of Islam -- and to destroy those who have destroyed us.

"Thou art our God, O Allah, and we are Thy people. Deliver us from our murderers and we will serve and obey Thee all the days of our life and we will teach our children Thy Praises and to submit to Thee for Thy Unequaled Love and Mercy for us.

"And thanks to You, O Allah, for making manifest our enemy (the devil), and help us, O Allah, to die the death of a Muslim."

Signed: Elijah Muhammad **Pgs. 330-341 MTBM**

Reference 15: Bowed To Golden Calf

Exodus 32:4

"He took what they handed him and made it into an idol cast in the shape of a calf, fashioning it with a tool. Then they said, 'These are your gods, Israel, who brought you up out of Egypt.'"

Both Jews and Christians are guilty of setting up rivals to Allah (God). Adam and Eve accepted the guidance of the serpent instead of that of Allah (Gen. 3:6). They made a golden calf and took it for their god and bowed down to it (Exod. 32:4). This was the work of their own hands to guide them and fight their wars. The Christians have made imaginary pictures and statues of wood, silver and gold -- calling them pictures and statues of God. They bow down to pictures and statues alleged to be of Jesus, His mother, and his disciples as though they could see and hear them. They (the Christians) claim sonship to Allah (God) and take the Son to be the equal of the Father, though they say "that they killed the Son." Today they take the weapons of war for their gods and put their trust in the work of their own hands.

Muhammad took hold of the best, the belief in one God (Allah), and was successful. Fourteen hundred years after him, we are successful, that is, we who will not set up another god with Allah. The fools who refuse to believe in Allah alone as the One God, if asked who made heaven and earth, most surely would say God and would say God the Son and the Holy Ghost. Then why do they not serve and obey Allah (God)?

It is a perfect insult to Allah (God) who made heaven and earth and makes the earth to produce everything for our service and even the sun, moon, and stars -- they serve our needs -- for us to bow down and worship anything other than Allah as a god. The Great Mahdi, Allah in person, who is in our midst today, will put a stop once and forever to the serving and worshiping of other gods besides Himself.

It is the devil's way of bringing the people (so-called Negroes) of Allah (God) in opposition to Him by teaching the people to believe and do just the thing that God forbids. Muhammad did not try making a likeness of God, nor have his followers done that. He and his followers obey the law of (the one God) Allah, while the Jews and the Christians preach it and do otherwise. We are now being brought face to face with Allah (God) for a showdown between Him and that which we have served as God besides Him. The lost and found members of the Asiatic nation are especially warned in the 112th chapter of the Holy Qur-an against the worship of any other god than Allah, for it is Allah in person who has found them among the worshipers of gods other than Allah. **Pgs. 74-75 MTBM**

Reference 16: Bring You Into Your Own Land

Ezekiel 36:24

"For I will take you out of the nations; I will gather you from all the countries and bring you back into your own land."

The Coming of the Son of Man, The Infidels are Angry *(Chapter from MTBM By The Honorable Mr. Elijah Muhammad)*

Who is the father if God is not His Father? God is His Father, but the Father is also a man. You have heard of old that God prepared a body, or the expected Son of Man; Jesus is a specially prepared man to do a work of redeeming the lost sheep (the so-called Negro). He had to have a body that would be part of each side (black and white), half and half. Therefore, being born or made from both people, He is able to go among both black and white without being discovered or recognized. This He has done in the person of Master W.F. Muhammad, the man who was made by His Father to go and search for the lost members of the Tribe of Shabazz. Master W.F. Muhammad is that Son of Man whom the world has been expecting to come for 2,000 years, seeking to save that which was lost. There are no historical records that there was ever a people lost from each other for 400 years other than we, the so-called Negroes. We have been so long separated from each other that we have lost the knowledge of each other. Even today the white American slave-masters are ever on the watch to keep out any Asiatic influence that might come among the so-called Negroes to teach them the truth. They are our real open enemies. This is no secret. The Son of Man is after the so-called Negroes to set them in Heaven and His enemies in hell. After His conquest of the black nation's enemies, the world will know and recognize

Him (Allah) to be God alone. There is no problem today that is as hard to solve as the problem of uniting the American so-called Negroes. They are like a dead man totally without life! They have lost all love of self and kind and have gone all out in loving their enemies. They do not seem to want any God to do anything like blessing them unless that God blesses their enemies too. Fear of their enemies is the real cause. The time is now ripe that they should have no fear, only the fear of Allah, Who is in person among them to save them from their enemies. By all means, they must be separated from the white race, in order that the scripture might be fulfilled. "For I will take you from among the heathen and gather you out of all countries and will bring you into your own land." (Ezek.36:24)

The so-called Negroes have no home that they can call their own. They have helped the white race to own a free country but they have nothing for themselves. This is the purpose of His coming, to give everyone that which is rightfully theirs. The Son of Man has power over all things. You cannot find a defense against Him in a war. Your weapons mean nothing. The power, of heaven and earth today will be ordered to fight on the side of the Mahdi against His enemies. He is the friend of the so-called Negroes and not of the white people. His purpose is to take the so-called Negroes and kill their enemies; although many of us will suffer from persecution and hunger. But, the good end is for those of you who will hold fast to Allah and His religion, Islam. They (the devils) cannot escape. Fly to Allah! Come, follow me. Although I may look insignificant to you, you will find salvation with us. The white race is excited and cannot think rightly for themselves. The so-called Negroes, Muslims, in their midst, are a shelter, but little do they know it. **Pgs. 19-21 MTBM**

Reference 17: Came From East

Matthew 24:27

"For as lightning that comes from the east is visible even in the west, so will be the coming of the Son of Man."

But the Bible teaches that God will be seen on the Day of Judgment. Not only the righteous will see Him, but even His enemies shall see Him.

On that day, a Son of a Man will sit to judge men according to their works. Who is the Father of this Son, coming to judge the world? Is His Father of flesh and blood or is He a "Spirit"? Where is this Son coming from? Prophet Jesus said "He will come from the East" (Matt 24:27), from the land and people of Islam, where all the former prophets came from. Jesus compared His coming as "the lightning". Of course lightning cannot be seen or heard at a great distance.

The actual light (the Truth) which "shineth even unto the West," is our day sun. But the Son of Man's coming is like both the lightning and our day sun. His work of the resurrection of the mentally dead so-called Negroes, and judgment between truth and falsehood, is compared with lightning on an instant. His swiftness in condemning the falsehood is like the sudden flash of lightning in a dark place. America is that dark place, where the darkness has blinded the people so that they cannot find the "right way" out. The sudden "flash of lightning" enables them to see that they are off from the "right path." They walk a few steps toward the "right way" but soon have to stop and wait for another bright flash. What they actually need is the light of the Sun (God in Person), that they may clearly see their way. The lightning does more than flash a light. It is also destructive striking whom Allah pleases, or taking property as well as lives. The brightness of its flashes almost blinds the eyes.

So it is with the coming of the Son of Man, with the truth, to cast it against falsehood that it breaks the head. Just a little hint of it makes the falsehood begin looking guilty and seeking cover from the brightness of the truth. Sometimes lightning serves as a warning of an approaching storm. So does Allah warn us by sending His Messengers with the truth, before the approaching destruction of a people to whom chastisement is justly due. They come flashing the truth in the midst of the spiritually darkened people. Those who love spiritual darkness will close their eyes to the flash of truth, like lightning, pointing out to them the "right way" thus blinding themselves from the knowledge of the approaching destruction of the storm of Allah, and are destroyed. "As the lightning cometh out of the East, so shall the coming of the Son of Man be."

Let us reflect on this prophecy from the direction in which this Son shall come, "out of the East." If He is to come from the East, to chastise or destroy that of the West, then He must be pleased with the East. The dominant religion of the East is Islam. The holy religious teachings of all the prophets, from Adam to Muhammad, was none other than Islam (Holy Qur-an 4:16), they all were of the East and came from that direction with the light of the Truth and shone toward the old wicked darkness of the West. But the West has ever closed its eyes and thus making it necessary for the coming of the Son of Man, the Great Mahdi, God in person.

Being the end of the signs, in His person, He dispels falsehood with the truth as the sun dispels night on its rising from the East. Why should the tribes of the earth mourn because of the coming of the Son of Man, instead of rejoicing? **Pgs. 12-13 MTBM**

Reference 18: Chastisement As Consequence Of Rejection

Revelation 21:8

"But the cowardly, the unbelieving, the vile, the murderers, the sexually immoral, those who practice magic arts, the idolaters and all liars—they will be consigned to the fiery lake of burning sulfur. This is the second death."

Reference 19: Chastisement As Consequence Of Rejection

Revelation 9:6

"During those days people will seek death but will not find it; they will long to die, but death will elude them."

Revelation 19:20

"But the beast was captured, and with it the false prophet who had performed the signs on its behalf. With these signs he had deluded those who had received the mark of the beast and worshiped its image. The two of them were thrown alive into the fiery lake of burning sulfur."

Reference 20: Chastisement As Consequence Of Rejection

Revelation 20:10

"And the devil, who deceived them, was thrown into the lake of burning sulfur, where the beast and the false prophet had been thrown. They will be tormented day and night for ever and ever."

Revelation 20:4

"I saw thrones on which were seated those who had been given authority to judge. And I saw the souls of those who had been beheaded because of their testimony about Jesus and because of the word of God. They had not worshiped the beast or its image and had not received its mark on their foreheads or their hands. They came to life and reigned with Christ a thousand years."

Revelation 20:15

"Anyone whose name was not found written in the book of life was thrown into the lake of fire."

TIME IS AT HAND
(Chapter from MTBM By The Honorable Mr. Elijah Muhammad)

Know that Allah is with us (the believers) and Allah has promised, in the Bible and in the Holy Qur-an, that if we believe and put our trust in Him, He is sufficient as a Protector, that no weapons formed against the true believers will prosper.

We are the true believers of Allah. As the Holy Qur-an teaches, they planned against us, but Allah also has plans, and He is the best of planners. I warn all of you that the devils, hypocrites and disbelievers will continue trying to turn you away from truth so you will have to suffer hellfire with them.

The so-called American Negroes (my people) are now in a time when they must decide on life or death. The world we have known is on its way out, and it wishes to carry you and me with it. But, it will not; this is the right path -- believe in Allah and come follow me.

We are the last members of the original Black Nation and have been found and chosen by Allah to make a great nation -- a nation under His guidance to excel the nations of the past.

Study the parable of Jesus and the lost sheep, the prodigal son (Luke 15:11, 21, 22), the stone that the builders rejected, the garden taken from the wicked husband and given to another and the mustard seed becoming a tree under which the beast found shade and in which the birds found rest.

Know that you, the so-called American Negroes, are divinely promised the Kingdom of Heaven (as it is called) after the destruction of this world. The people of this world will stop at nothing in trying to seduce you to follow them and remain with them so that you, too, will share in their doom. They ask you to take part in their doom, and you accept. When accepting the call to their false friendship you are accepting death.

I hope you remember what I said to you concerning the prepared destruction of Allah for this people and you who take part with them. Since they already have a head start, they believe they will deceive you in going along with them, ignoring the call of Allah and your own salvation and heaven at once while you live.

The consequence of this rejection of His call will get you a disgraceful year's punishment or chastisement (night and day). You will wish that you were dead. When night comes, you will wish it were day, and when day comes, you will wish it night. You can find this chastisement mentioned in Revelation (Rev. 9:6; 19:20; 20:10, 14, 15, and 21:8).

Salvation has come to the black men of America, but their fear of losing the hate -- I cannot say the love because they do not love you -- of their enemies causes them to reject it.

Within 24 months, every one of you who is now a disbeliever in Allah and the great brotherhood of Islam will be suffering the punishments that have been mentioned in the above chapters and verses.

America is the first country and people that Allah wishes to destroy, but he will not destroy them until you have heard the truth of her and of yourself. I shall continue to warn you of the divine penalty that awaits you who reject your God and my Saviour, Master Fard Muhammad. In this world of crisis and destruction of nations, the only escape you have is in Allah and following me.
Pg. 297 MTBM

Reference 21: Come Out Of Her

Revelation 18:4

"Then I heard another voice from heaven say: 'Come out of her, my people, so that you will not share in her sins, so that you will not receive any of her plagues.'"

The black people, and especially the so-called Negroes, are now in the very area where God has said to me that the fire (often referred to as the "fire of hell" or "hell fire") will begin which will destroy the present wicked white race of America first. The sins of the white race are far worse and more pungent to the nostril of God than the sins of Sodom and Gomorrah! The fire of hell is not intended for the so-called Negroes: only those who, after hearing this teaching of the truth which I am giving to you and the warnings of Allah (God), will willfully hold on to the white race and their religion, Christianity.

The so-called Negroes are made so poisoned by this wicked race of devils that they love them more than they love their own people. It is really because of the evil done to them by the American white race that Allah (God) has put them on His list, as the first to be destroyed. The others will be given a little longer to live, as the prophet Daniel says (7:11, 19 and Rev. 19:20). Believe it, or let it alone, the above refers to America. She is the only white government out of the European race that answers the description of the symbolic Fourth Beast. The so-called Negroes are warned to come out of her (America) (Rev. 18:4), though the truth of Daniel and Revelations could not be told until the time of the end of this prophecy.

The Bible means good if you can rightly understand it. My interpretation of it is given to me from the Lord of the Worlds. Yours is your own and from the enemies of the truth. The so-called Negroes will be the lucky ones, that is, if they stop following and practicing the evils and indecent doings of this wicked and doomed race of devils (whose true self has been a secret for 6,000 years).

So-called Negroes, accept your own God, religion and people so that you may be successful in escaping the fire! **Pg. 88 MTBM**

Reference 22: Coming of God

Habakkuk Chapter 3

A prayer of Habakkuk the prophet. On shigionoth.

"Lord, I have heard of your fame; I stand in awe of your deeds, Lord. Repeat them in our day, in our time make them known; in wrath remember mercy."

"God came from Teman, the Holy One from Mount Paran. His glory covered the heavens and his praise filled the earth."

"His splendor was like the sunrise; rays flashed from his hand, where his power was hidden."

"Plague went before him; pestilence followed his steps."

"He stood, and shook the earth; he looked, and made the nations tremble. The ancient mountains crumbled and the age-old hills collapsed—but he marches on forever."

"I saw the tents of Cushan in distress, the dwellings of Midian in anguish."

"Were you angry with the rivers, Lord? Was your wrath against the streams? Did you rage against the sea when you rode your horses and your chariots to victory?"

"You uncovered your bow, you called for many arrows. You split the earth with rivers."

"The mountains saw you and writhed. Torrents of water swept by; the deep roared and lifted its waves on high."

"Sun and moon stood still in the heavens at the glint of your flying arrows, at the lightning of your flashing spear."

"In wrath you strode through the earth and in anger you threshed the nations."

"You came out to deliver your people, to save your anointed one. You crushed the leader of the land of wickedness, you stripped him from head to foot."

"With his own spear you pierced his head when his warriors stormed out to scatter us, gloating as though about to devour the wretched who were in hiding."

"You trampled the sea with your horses, churning the great waters."

"I heard and my heart pounded, my lips quivered at the sound; decay crept into my bones, and my legs trembled. Yet I will wait patiently for the day of calamity to come on the nation invading us."

"Though the fig tree does not bud and there are no grapes on the vines, though the olive crop fails and the fields produce no food, though there are no sheep in the pen and no cattle in the stalls..."

"Yet I will rejoice in the Lord, I will be joyful in God my Savior."

"The Sovereign Lord is my strength; he makes my feet like the feet of a deer, he enables me to tread on the heights."

For the director of music. On my stringed instruments.

Reference 105: Teman, A Son Of Esau

Genesis 36:11
"The sons of Eliphaz: Teman, Omar, Zepho, Gatam, and Kenaz."

Genesis 36:15
"These were the chiefs among Esau's descendants: The sons of Eliphaz, Esau's firstborn: Chiefs Teman, Omar, Zepho, Kenaz."

Genesis 36:42
"Kenaz, Teman, Mibzar, Magdiel, and Iram. These were the chiefs of Edom, according to their settlements in the land they occupied. This is the family line of Esau, the father of the Edomites."

Reference 114: Thy People

Habakkuk 3:13

"You came out to deliver your people, to save your anointed one. You crushed the leader of the land of wickedness, you stripped him from head to foot."

Reference 122: Work Of God Against Enemy

Habakkuk 3

A prayer describing God's power and His actions against the nations to save His people. (Read This Chapter)

The Coming of God: Is He a Man or a Spirit?
(Chapter from MTBM By The Honorable Mr. Elijah Muhammad)

According to the dictionary of the Bible: Teman, a son of Esau by Adah (Gen. 36:11, 15, 42) and in I Chron. 1:36, now if Habakkuk saw God come or coming from the sons of Esau (Eliphaz), then God must be a man and not a spook. If Habakkuk's (3:3) prophecy refers to some country, town, or city, if there be any truth at all in this prophecy, then we can say that this prophet saw God as a material being, belonging to the human family of the earth--and not to a spirit (ghost). In the same chapter and verse, Habakkuk saw the Holy One from Mount Paran. This is also earthly, somewhere in Arabia. Here the Bible makes a difference between God and another person who is called the Holy One. Which one should we take for our God? For one is called God, while another One is called Holy One. The Holy One: His glory covered the heavens and the earth was full of His praise.

It has been a long time since the earth was full of praise for a Holy One. Even to this hour, the people do not care for Holy

People and will persecute and kill the Holy One, if God does not intervene. In the fourth verse of the above chapter, it says, "He had horns coming out of his hands: and there was the hiding of His power." Such science to represent the God's power could confuse the ignorant masses of the world. Two gods are here represented at the same time. (It is good that God makes Himself manifest to the ignorant world today.) "The burning coals, went forth at His feet," has a meaning but what is the meaning? The ignorant do not know. "The burning coals" could refer to the anger and war among the people where His foot trod within the borders of the wicked. (Here God has feet--Spirits do not have feet and hands.)

This Holy One does not refer to anyone of the past- not Moses, Jesus or Mohammed of the past 1300 years. "For this Holy One the perpetual hills did bow. Cushan in affliction; the curtains of the land of Midian did tremble." (What is meant by the curtains trembling?) (Who is Cushan?) "The mountains saw thee, they trembled. (What does this mean?) "The sun and moon stood still in their habitation." (What does this mean?)

The answers to the above questions are easy when we understand who this God called the Holy One coming from Mount Paran is. The 13th verse should clear the way for such undertaking; for it tells us why all these great things took place on the coming of the Holy One from Mount Paran. It says: "Thou wentest forth for the salvation of thy people (not for all people) for the salvation with thine anointed (His Apostle). He wounded the head out of the house of the wicked by discovering the foundation unto the neck (by exposing the truth and ruling powers of the wicked race of devils,)"

"Cushan" represents the Black Nation which is afflicted by the white race. "The curtains of the land of Midian" could mean the falsehood spread over the people by the white race and their leaders trembling from being exposed by the truth. "The mountains" represent the great, rich and powerful political men of the wicked; they also are trembling and being divided and scattered over the earth. "The Holy One" is God in person and not a spirit! **Pgs. 7-8 MTBM**

Reference 23: Coming Of Son Of Man

Matthew 24:27
"For as lightning that comes from the east is visible even in the west, so will be the coming of the Son of Man."

THE COMING OF THE SON OF MAN, THE GREAT MAHDI
(Chapter from MTBM By The Honorable Mr. Elijah Muhammad)

"For as the lightning cometh out of the East, and shineth even unto the West, so shall the coming of the Son of Man be."
(Matt. 24:27)

My greatest and only desire is to bring true understanding of the word of God, His prophets and the scriptures, which the prophets were sent with, pertaining to the lost-found people (the American so-called Negroes) of God and the judgment of the world.

You must forget about ever seeing the return of Jesus, Who was here 2,000 years ago. Set your heart on seeing the One that He prophesied would come at the end of the present world's time (the while race's time).

He is called the "Son of Man," the "Christ," the "Comforter." You are really foolish to be looking to see the return of the Prophet Jesus. It is the same as looking for the return of Abraham, Moses and Muhammad. All of these prophets prophesied the coming of Allah or one with equal power, under many names. You must remember that Jesus could not have been referring to Himself as returning to the people in the last days. He prophesied of another's coming who was much greater than He. Jesus even acknowledged that He did not know when the hour would come in these words; "But of that day and hour knoweth no man, no, not the angels of heaven, but my Father only." (Matt. 24:36).

If He were the one to return at the end of the world, surely He would have had knowledge of the time of His return, the knowledge of the hour. But He left Himself out of No that knowledge and placed it where it belonged, as all the others— prophets— had done. No prophet has been able to tell us the hour of the judgment. No one but He, the great all wise God, Allah. He is called the "Son of Man," the "Mahdi", the "Christ". The prophets, Jesus included, could only foretell those things which would serve as signs, signs that would precede such a great one's coming to judge the world. The knowledge of the hour of judgment is with the Executor only.

The prophets teach us to let the past judgments of people, their cities, and their warner's serve as a lesson, or sign of the last judgment and its warner's. Noah did not know the hour of the flood. Lot did not know the Hour of Sodom and Gomorrah until the Executors had arrived, and Jesus prophesied; (Matt.24:37-39), "it will be the same in the last judgment of the world of Satan." You have gone astray because of your misunderstanding of the scripture, the Prophet Jesus, and the coming of God to judge the world. My corrections are not accepted.

Your misunderstanding and misinterpretation of it is really the joy of devils. For it is the devils' desire to keep the so-called Negroes ignorant of the truth of God until they see it with their eyes. The truth of God is the salvation and freedom of the so called Negroes from the devils' power.

Can you blame them? No! Blame yourself for being so foolish as to allow the devils to fool you in not accepting the truth after it comes to you. The devils have tried to deceive the people all over the earth with Christianity, that is, God the Father, Jesus the Son, the Holy Ghost; three Gods into One God. The resurrection of the Son and His return to judge the world; or that the Son is in some place above the earth, sitting on the right-hand side of the Father, waiting until the Father makes His enemies His footstool. The period of waiting is 2,000 years. Yet, He died for the Father to save His enemies (the whole world of sinners).

My friends, use a bit of common sense. First, could a wonderful flesh and blood body, made of the essence of our earth, last 2,000 years on the earth, or off the earth, without being healed! Second, where exists such a heaven, of the earth, that flesh and blood of the earth can exist, since the Bible teaches that flesh and blood cannot enter heaven? (Cor. 15:50)

Flesh and blood cannot survive without that of which it is made, the earth. Jesus' prophesy of the coming of the Son of Man is very clear, if you rightly understand. First, this removes all doubt about who we should expect to execute judgment, for if man is to be judged and rewarded according to his actions, who could be justified in sitting as judge of man's doings but another man? How could a spirit be our judge when we cannot see a spirit? And ever since life was created, life has had spirit. But the Bible teaches that God will be seen on the Day of Judgment. Not only the righteous will see Him, but even His enemies shall see Him.

On that day, a Son of a Man will sit to judge men according to their works. Who is the Father of this Son, coming to judge the world? Is His Father of flesh and blood or is He a "Spirit"? Where is this Son coming from? Prophet Jesus said "He will come from the East" (Matt 24:27), from the land and people of Islam, where all the former prophets came from. Jesus compared His coming as "the lightning". Of course lightning cannot be seen or heard at a great distance.

The actual light (the Truth) which "shineth even unto the West," is our day sun. But the Son of Man's coming is like both the lightning and our day sun. His work of the resurrection of the mentally dead so-called Negroes, and judgment between truth and falsehood, is compared with lightning on an instant. His swiftness in condemning the falsehood is like the sudden flash of lightning in a dark place. America is that dark place, where the darkness has blinded the people so that they cannot find the "right way" out. The sudden "flash of lightning" enables them to see that they are off from the "right path." They walk a few steps toward the "right way" but soon have to stop and wait for another bright flash. What they actually need is the light of the Sun (God in Person), that they may clearly see their way. The lightning does more than flash a light. It is also destructive striking whom Allah pleases, or taking property as well as lives. The brightness of its flashes almost blinds the eyes.

So it is with the coming of the Son of Man, with the truth, to cast it against falsehood that it breaks the head. Just a little hint of it makes the falsehood begin looking guilty and seeking cover from the brightness of the truth. Sometimes lightning serves as a warning of an approaching storm. So does Allah warn us by sending His Messengers with the truth, before the approaching destruction of a people to whom chastisement is justly due. They come flashing the truth in the midst of the spiritually darkened people. Those who love spiritual darkness will close their eyes to the flash of truth, like lightning, pointing out to them the "right way" thus blinding themselves from the knowledge of the approaching destruction of the storm of Allah, and are destroyed. "As the lightning cometh out of the East, so shall the coming of the Son of Man be."

Let us reflect on this prophecy from the direction in which this Son shall come, "out of the East." If He is to come from the East, to chastise or destroy that of the West, then He must be pleased with the East. The dominant religion of the East is Islam. The holy religious teachings of all the prophets, from Adam to Muhammad, was none other than Islam (Holy Qur-an 4:16), they all were of the East and came from that direction with the light of the Truth and shone toward the old wicked darkness of the West. But the West has ever closed its eyes and thus making it necessary for the coming of the Son of Man, the Great Mahdi, God in person.

Being the end of the signs, in His person, He dispels falsehood with the truth as the sun dispels night on its rising from the East. Why should the tribes of the earth mourn because of the coming of the Son of Man, instead of rejoicing? **Pgs. 10-13 MTBM**

Reference 24: Created Them In His Image

Genesis 1:27

"So God created mankind in his own image, in the image of God he created them; male and female he created them."

God created them in His image (Gen. 1:27). They are in the image and likeness of a human being (black man), but are altogether different kind of human being than that of the black human beings.

Their pale white skin; their blue eyes (even disliked by themselves) tells any black man or woman, that in those blue and green eyes, there just can't be any sincere love and friendship for them. They are unlike and we are like. Like repels -- unlike attracts. The very characteristics of black and white are so very different.

Black people have a heart of gold, love and mercy. Such a heart, nature did not give to the white race. This is where the so-called Negroes are deceived in this devil race. They think they have the same kind of heart; but the white race knows better. They have kept it as a secret among themselves, that they may be able to deceive the black people.

They have been, and still are, successful in deceiving the black man, under the disguise of being the ones who want peace, love and friendship with the world, and with God -- at the same time making war with the world, to destroy peace, love and friendship of the black nation.

A brother loves and desires for his brother what he desires for himself. So-called Negroes, do you have this kind of love and desire from the white race for you? Why? Because as I have shown to you, they are not your brothers, by nature. They are fully showing you, this day, openly, that they are different from you; and, you are different from them.

Why not try making brotherly love and friendship with your own kind first? To see you trying to integrate with the very enemy of yours, and God, shows beyond a shadow of a doubt, that you don't know yourself nor your enemies; or rather are lost in love for our enemies, I know you, who love your enemy, don't like that I tell you this truth. But, I can't help it--come what may. God has put upon me this mission, and I must do His will or burn.

Are you with me to do the will of God, or will of the devil and the disbelieving people? I know you are, for you have learned and are learning more truth than you have ever read or ever will read. Fear not! Allah is on our side, to give you and me the Kingdom. **Pgs. 121-122 MTBM**

Reference 25: Creating A Race

Genesis 1:26

"Then God said, 'Let us make mankind in our image, in our likeness, so that they may rule over the fish in the sea and the birds in the sky, over the livestock and all the wild animals, and over all the creatures that move along the ground.'"

The original man, Allah has declared, is none other than the black man. The black man is the first and the last, maker and owner of the universe. From him came all brown, yellow, red and white people. By using a special method of birth control law the black man was able to produce the white race.

The true knowledge of the Black and white mankind should be enough to awaken the so-called Negroes and put them on their feet and on the road to self-independence. Yet, they are so afraid of the slave-masters that they even love them to their destruction and wish that the bearer of truth would not tell the truth even if he knows it.

The time has arrived when it must be told the world over. There are millions who do not know who is the original man. Why should this question be put before the world today? Because it is the time of judgement between the black and white and the knowledge of the rightful owners of the earth.

Allah is now pointing out to the nations of earth their rightful places, and this judgement will bring an end to war over it. Now it is so easy to recognize the original man, the real owner of the earth, by the history of the two (black and white). We have an unending past history of the black nation and a limited one of the white race.

We find that history teaches that the earth was populated by the black nation ever since it was created, but the history of the white race does not take us beyond 6,000 years.

Everywhere the white race has gone on our planet, they have either found the original man or a sign that he had been there previously. Allah is proving to the world of black men that the white race actually does not own any part of our planet.

The Bible and the Holy Qur'an bears witness to the above, if you are able to understand it. The Holy Qur'an, the beauty of Scriptures, repeatedly challenges the white race to point out the part of the heavens and the earth that they created.

It further teaches that they are not even their own creators. We created white man from a small life germ, the soft pronoun "we" used nearly throughout the Holy Qur'an makes the knowledge of the original man much clearer and more intelligent of how the white race's creation took place.

In the Bible, referring to their creation, we have US (Gen. 1:26) creating, or rather making the race; the US and WE used show beyond a shadow of a doubt that they came from another people. **Pgs. 53-54 MTBM**

Again, we learn who the Bible (Genesis 1:26) is referring to in the saying: Let us make man. This US was fifty-nine thousand, nine hundred and ninety-nine (59,999) black men and women; making or grafting them into the likeness or image of the original man.

Now that they are the same, but have the ways of a human being they are referred to as mankind -- not the real original man, but a being made like the original in the sense of human beings.

The Holy Qur-an throws a great light on the truth of the creation of this pale, white race of devils. O mankind, surely we have created you from a male and a female (Chap. 49:15). This makes it very easy to understand to whom it is referring. What mankind? Surely we created man from sperm mixed (with ovum) to try him, so we have made him hearing and seeing. (Chap. 76:2).

Inasmuch as these chapters have a further reference to the spiritual creation of the Last Messenger, it is equally true that they refer to the physical creation of the white race. In another place, the Holy Qur-an says: We have created man, and now he is an open disputer. **Pgs. 118-119 MTBM**

Reference 26: Curse Of Noah

Genesis 9:21-25

"When he drank some of its wine, he became drunk and lay uncovered inside his tent. Ham, the father of Canaan, saw his father naked and told his two brothers outside. But Shem and Japheth took a garment and laid it across their shoulders; then they walked in backward and covered their father's naked body..."

"When Noah awoke from his wine and found out what his youngest son had done to him, he said, 'Cursed be Canaan! The lowest of slaves will he be to his brothers.'"

"But the day of the Lord will come like a thief. The heavens will disappear with a roar; the elements will be destroyed by fire, and the earth and everything done in it will be laid bare."

The original scripture called "The Torah" -- revealed to Musa (Moses) -- was Holy until the Jews and the Christian scholars started tampering with it. Today, the Bible has become a "commercialized book," therefore, many are allowed to rewrite or revise it. I think when it comes to the word of Allah (God) or a book revealed by Him, that word or book is sacred and should be protected from corruption by the hands of people who care nothing for its sacredness. It is like a "rattlesnake" in the hands of my people, for they (most of them) do not understand it.

Some believe (in that story of the Bible) that the black people are a curse of Noah on one of his sons (Ham) because this son laughed at his father's nakedness while being drunk from wine (Genesis 9:21-25). The black nation has no birth record. There were as many or more black people on our planet in the days of Noah as there are today. The Bible's record of the flood is 2,348 years before Christ, and if the records are true, we are nearly 4,500 years from Noah's flood. If there were no black people before Noah, then that wicked people who were destroyed in the flood were white people. And again, if those were of that race, the warning of the destruction of the wicked world by fire the next time is made clearer to those whom that fire will destroy. **Pgs. 87-88 MTBM**

Reference 27: Dan Shall Be A Serpent

Genesis 49:17

"Dan will be a snake by the roadside, a viper along the path, that bites the horse's heels so that its rider tumbles backward."

That old serpent, called the devil and Satan, which deceiveth the whole world (Rev. 12:9) is a person or persons whose characteristics are like that of a serpent (snake). Serpents or snakes of the grafted type cannot be trusted, for they will strike you when you are not expecting a strike.

Let us refer to Genesis: Dan shall be a serpent by the way, an adder in the path that bitten the horse's heels so that his rider shall fall backward (Gen. 49:17). Here Jacob on his deathbed foretelleth the future of his sons (Moses calls Dan a lion's whelp; he shall leap from Basin; Duet. 33:22). That old serpent, devil and Satan, the old beast, is the dragon which deceiveth the whole world of the poor ignorant darker nations and has caused them to fall off their mount of prosperity, success and independence by accepting advice, guidance and empty promises which he (the serpent-like Caucasian devil) never intended to fulfill.

How well the prophets have described the characteristics of this race of devils as corresponding to the nature of a snake (serpent). Most snakes wobble and make a crooked trail when and wherever they crawl. So it is with the white race, which goes among the black nation leaving the marks of evil and crooked dealings and doings.

In spiritual dealings, there again you will find them like a snake (serpent), following on the heels of the truth bearers (prophets and messengers of God) to bite the believers with false teachings and fear in order that he may cause them to fall off their mount of truth. Like a snake (serpent) he parks in and on the pathway of all the so-called Negroes who seek the way to freedom, truth, justice and equality (Allah and the true religion, Islam). In many instances, they threaten you with imprisonment the loss of your jobs, hunger, lack of shelter and disrespect of human rights. On some occasions, they threaten to take away your very life! By speaking evil of the truth (Allah and His apostle and Islam), they cause fear to enter the hearts of the weak believers and they fall off the mount of the truth of God which would have saved them from fear, harm, hunger and lack of shelter. As he caused the fall of Adam and his wife from the Garden of Paradise, so they are trying to cause the fall of you and me and prevent us from entering Paradise by not believing in Allah and His religion, Islam. **Pgs. 122-123 MTBM**

Reference 28: Darkness Was Open

Genesis 1:2

"Now the earth was formless and empty, darkness was over the surface of the deep, and the Spirit of God was hovering over the waters."

The Bible is now being called the Poison Book by God Himself, and who can deny that it is not poison? It has poisoned the very hearts and minds of the so-called Negroes so much that they can't agree with each other. From the first day that the white race received the Divine Scripture they started tampering with its truth to make it suit themselves, and blind the black man. It is their nature to do evil, and the Book can't be recognized as the pure and Holy Word of God. It opens with the words of someone other than God trying to represent God and His Creation to us. This is called the Book of Moses and reads as follows: In the beginning God created Heaven and Earth (Gen. 1:1). When was this beginning? There in the Genesis the writer tells us that it was 4,004 B.C.. This we know, now, that it refers to the making of the white race, and not the heavens and earth. The second verse of the first chapter of Genesis reads: And the earth was without form and void; darkness was upon the deep and the spirit of God moved upon the face of the waters. What was the water on, since there was no form of earth? As I see it, the Bible is very questionable. After God had created everything without asking anyone for help then comes His weakness in the 26th verse of the same chapter (Gen. 1:26). He invites us to help Him make a man. Allah has revealed "the us" that was invited to make a man (white race). A man is far more easy to make than the heavens and earth. We can't charge these questionable readings of the Bible to Musa because he was a prophet of God, and they don't lie.

If the present Bible is the direct Word of God, why isn't God speaking rather than His Prophet Musa (Moses)? Neither does Moses tell us here in the first chapter of Genesis that it is from God. No, we don't find the name Moses mentioned in the chapter. The Bible is the graveyard of my poor people (the so-called Negroes) and I would like to dwell upon this book until I am sure they understand that it is not quite as holy as they thought it was. I don't mean to say that there is no truth in it; certainly there is plenty of truth, if understood. Will you accept the understanding of it? The Bible charges all of its Great Prophets will evil, it makes God guilty of an act of adultery by charging Him with being the father of Mary's baby (Jesus), again it charges Noah and Lot with drunkenness, and Lot with getting children by his daughter. What a Poison Book. **Pgs. 94-95 MTBM**

"The journey to understanding is not meant to be traveled alone. Our community welcomes those who seek knowledge and are ready to engage in meaningful discussions about these teachings. Join us and connect with others who are committed to the truth."

 https://nwnoicommunity.aitribes.app/ft/axkVr)

Reference 29: Day Of The Lord

2 Peter 3:10

"But the day of the Lord will come like a thief. The heavens will disappear with a roar; the elements will be destroyed by fire, and the earth and everything done in it will be laid bare."

American whites want us to reject Allah and the true religion, Islam and believe in their false religion and false god, whom they cannot make manifest to you. They cannot prove to you in this day and time that Christianity is a defense for you as well as for themselves against their doom.

America must be taken and destroyed according to the prophets, at the time and end of the wicked world, where the lost and found members of the ancient and aboriginal people are found, America hates and mistreats her slaves to the extent that it has reached the heart of Allah and the righteousness of the people of the earth (the Nation of Islam).

We read where our black brothers refer to the American so-called Negroes as their brothers, while according to the preachings of some of these lost and found members of the aboriginal nation of the earth they would rather have themselves referred to as the brothers of their enemies.

The extent to which the enemy has poisoned the minds and hearts of my people here in America is shameful. They willfully do anything to deceive the so-called Negroes into going to their doom with them. There is no way for the enemy of Allah, His Messenger and His people (the darker people of the earth) to find strength, power and wisdom enough to win in a war against Allah. As it is written in the Christian Bible and many other places: "But the day of the Lord will come as a thief in the night; in thee, which the heavens shall pass away with a great noise and the elements shall melt with fervent heat, the earth also and the works that are therein shall be burned up" (2 Peter 3:10).

The earth shall not be burned; it will be here for many thousands of years to come. Only that on the earth (the devils) which has sinned against Allah and His laws will be destroyed. The earth, the sun, the moon and the stars have never disobeyed Allah since their creation. **Pgs. 280-281 MTBM**

Reference 30: Day Of The Lord Is Near

Joel 3:14

"Multitudes, multitudes in the valley of decision! For the day of the Lord is near in the valley of decision."

Since 1492, the people of the white race have been allowed to spread over the face of the earth (to have the freedom of deceiving all that they could). To learn more about them, let us read and study their history. Read in the Bible the Revelation of John, under the title of "The Beast and the Dragon."

Their history shows trouble-making, murder and death to all darker people from the far-off islands and mainlands of Asia as well as the South Seas and the Pacific and Atlantic Oceans. All have been touched by their destructive hand and evil way of civilization and finally the bringing of my people to make their destruction sure.

Actually it was suicide for them to have brought our fathers in slavery. This act was charged to them by the Divine Supreme Being as being the most wicked people on the earth. Now we see the results in the fight of the ignorant among our people to gain sincere love from a people who have no sincere love among themselves.

They have never practiced sincere love, according to their own history of war making, robbery, murder and exploitation among themselves. This is clear to you who see and understand.

The so-called Negro has been made so blind, deaf and dumb by them that even the intellectual blacks now are blind and seek to make love and friendship with the people of the devil and satan. The day of decision between the dark races or nations was begun by God Himself in the Person of Master Fard Muhammad, to Whom be praised forever, as is prophesied in the Bible: "Multitudes in the valley of decision, for the day [before or by 1970] of the Lord is near in the valley of decision" (Joel 3:14). **Pgs. 267-268**

Reference 31: Deceive Nations

2 Thessalonians 2:9-10

"The coming of the lawless one will be in accordance with how Satan works. He will use all sorts of displays of power through signs and wonders that serve the lie, and all the ways that wickedness deceives those who are perishing..."

For thousands of years, the people who did not have the Knowledge of the person, or reality of God worshiped their own

Ideas of God. He has been made like many things other than what He really is. The Christians refer to God as a "Mystery" and a "Spirit" and divide Him into thirds. One part they call the Father, another part the Son, and the third part they call the Holy Ghost; which makes the three, one. This is contrary to both nature and mathematics. The law of mathematics will not allow us to put three into one. Our nature rebels against such a belief of God being a mystery and yet the Father of a son and a Holy Ghost without a wife or without being something In reality. We wonder how can the son be human, and the father a mystery (unknown), or a spirit? Who is this Holy Ghost that is classified as being the equal of the father and the son?

The Christians do not believe in God as being a human being, yet they believe in Him as being the Father of all human beings. They also refer to God as He, Him, Man, King and The Ruler. They teach that God sees, hears, talks, walks, stands, sits, rides, and flies; that He grieves or sorrows; and that He is interested in the affairs of human beings. They also teach that once upon a time He made the first man like Himself in the image and likeness of Himself, but yet they believe that He, Himself, is not a man or human. They preach and prophesy of His coming and that He will be seen on the Judgment Day but is not man. They cannot tell us what He looks like, yet man is made like Him and in the image of God, and yet they still say that He is a mystery (unknown).

How can one teach the people to know God if He, himself, does not know God. If you try teaching the Christians that God is also a human being, they will say that you are crazy, that you do not believe in God and that you are an infidel. In the meantime, while they admit that He is a Mystery God (unknown), they teach not to make any likeness of Him; yet they adorn their walls and churches with pictures, images and statues like human beings.

Can God be a Mystery God and yet send prophets to represent Himself? Have the prophets been representing a God that is not known (Mystery)? They tell us that they heard Gods voice speaking to them in their own language. Can a spirit speak a language while being an immaterial something? If God is not material, what pleasure would He get out of material beings and the material universe? What is the basis of spirit? Is the spirit independent of material?

Actually, who is that Mystery God? We should take time and study what has and is being taught to us. Study the word and examine it, and if it be the Truth, lay hold to it. To teach people that God is a Mystery God is to teach them that God is unknown. There is no truth in such teaching. Can one teach that which he himself does not know?

If one teaches a thing that he himself does not know, he can be charged with lying to the people. The word "mystery," according to the English dictionaries, is something that has not been or cannot be - something beyond human comprehension. The unintelligent, or rather ones without divine knowledge, seem to delight themselves in representing the God as something mysterious Unknown.

Such teaching (a mystery God) that God is a mystery makes the prophets' teachings of God all false. There should be a law made and enforced upon such teachers until they have been removed from the public.

According to Allah, the origin of such teachings as a Mystery God is from the devils! It was taught to them by their father, Yakub, 6,000 years ago. They know today that God is not a mystery but will not teach it. He (devil), the god of evil, was made to rule the nations of earth for 6,000 years, and naturally he would not teach obedience to a God other than himself.

So, a knowledge of the true God of Righteousness was not represented by the devils. The true God was not to be made manifest to the people until the god of evil (devil) has finished or lived out his time, which was allowed to deceive the nations (read These. 2:9-10, Rev. 20:3, 8-10). **Pgs. 1-2 MTBM**

Reference 32: Delivered Jonah

Jonah 2:2-4

"In my distress I called to the Lord, and he answered me. From deep in the realm of the dead I called for help, and you listened to my cry. You hurled me into the depths, into the very heart of the seas, and the currents swirled about me; all your waves and breakers swept over me..."

"Glory to Thee, O Allah, and Thine is the praise. Blessed is Thy name and exalted is Thy majesty and there is none to be served besides Thee. I betake me for refuge to Allah against the accursed devil."

Study the words of the Muslim's prayers and try finding anything to equal them in any other religion. The Christians have no intelligent prayer service set forth in the Bible. There is no mention of God teaching Adam to pray. Jesus set forth only one prayer to His disciples and did not appoint any certain time to recite it.

The following is the oft-repeated prayer of the Muslims:

"In the name of Allah, the Beneficent, the Merciful; all praise is due to Allah, the Lord of the worlds, the Beneficent, the Merciful, Master of the day of requital. Thee do we serve and Thee do we beseech for help. Guide us on the right path of those upon whom Thou hast bestowed favors, not of those upon whom Thy wrath is brought down, nor of those who go astray. Amen."

What a good prayer for one who is lost from the right direction as the so-called Negroes are to pray. They (the white race) cannot regain paradise because they are not members of that family. But, on the other hand, the lost-found so-called Negroes are really, by nature, members of the original family of paradise. It was by prayer and the turning in the right direction (toward the Holy Temple Mecca) that delivered Jonah from the belly of the fish (Jonah 2:2-4) which is only a type of us here in America (the anti-typical fish) who has swallowed us.

Our prayers will be speedily heard and Allah will fight our battles against our enemies and bring them to disgrace. **Pgs. 140-141 MTBM**

Reference 33: Devil Deceived People Of Paradise

Genesis 3:13

"Then the Lord God said to the woman, 'What is this you have done?' The woman said, 'The serpent deceived me, and I ate.'"

Reference 35: Devil Kill Own Brother

Genesis 4:8

"Now Cain said to his brother Abel, 'Let's go out to the field.' While they were in the field, Cain attacked his brother Abel and killed him."

THE BLOOD SHEDDER
(Chapter from MTBM By The Honorable Mr. Elijah Muhammad)

According to the word of Allah (God) and the history of the world, since the grafting of the Caucasian race 6,000 years ago, they have caused more bloodshed than any people known to the black nation. Born murderers, their very nature is to murder. The Bible and Holy Qur-an Sharrieff are full of teachings of this bloody race of devils. They shed the life blood of all life, even their own, and are scientists at deceiving the black people.

They deceived the very people of Paradise (Bible, Gen. 3:13). They killed their own brother (Gen. 4:8). The innocent earth's blood (Gen. 4:10) revealed it to its Maker (thy brother's blood cryeth unto me from the ground). The very earth, the soil of America, soaked with the innocent blood of the so-called Negroes shed by this race of devils, now crieth out to its Maker for her burden of carrying the innocent blood of the righteous slain upon her. Let us take a look at the devil's creation from the teaching of the Holy Qur-an.

And when your Lord said to the angels, I am going to place in the earth one who shall rule, the angels said: What will Thou place in it such as shall make mischief in it and shed blood, we celebrate Thy praise and extol Thy holiness (Holy Qur-an Sharrieff 2:30).

This devil race has and still is doing just that -- making mischief and shedding blood of the black nation whom they were grafted from. Your Lord said to the angels, "Surely I am going to create a mortal of the essence of black mud fashioned in shape" (Holy Qur-an Sharrieff, 15:28).

The essence of black mud (the black nation) mentioned is only symbolic, which actually means the sperm of the black nation, and they refused to recognize the black nation as their equal though they were made from and by a black scientist (named Yakub). They can never see their way in submitting to Allah and the religion Islam and His prophets.

The slave-masters' every cry is to beat- beat- kill- kill- the so-called Negroes. Maybe the day has arrived that Allah will return to the devils -- that which they have been so anxious to pour on the poor innocent so-called Negroes. Allah will give you your own blood to drink like water and your arms and allies will not help you against him (Rev. 16:6).

The heads and bodies of the so-called Negroes are used to test the clubs and guns of the devils, and yet the poor, foolish, so-called Negroes admire the devils regardless to how they are treated.

America is now under Divine Plagues. One will come after the other until she is destroyed. Allah has said it. **Pgs. 128-129 MTBM**

Reference 34: Devil Deceived The Woman

Revelation 12:4

"Its tail swept a third of the stars out of the sky and flung them to the earth. The dragon stood in front of the woman who was about to give birth, so that it might devour her child the moment he was born."

THE BEAST PART II
WHO IS ABLE TO MAKE WAR WITH HIM?
(Chapter from MTBM By The Honorable Mr. Elijah Muhammad)

Who is able to make war with him? (Rev. 13:4)
dreadful and terrible (Dan. 7:7)

God and His Prophets could not have given the white race a better name (serpent) according to the characteristics of that race. The serpent of Genesis 3:1 was none other than the devil (white race). He deceived Adam and his wife, causing them to disobey Allah (God), which was the plan of the serpent (devil), according to the history of the devils. Their greatest desire is to make the righteous disobey the law of righteousness.

They are referred to by this name serpent in the Holy Qur-an (37:65) translated by Maulvi Muhammad Ali: To a tree that grows in the bottom of hell, its produce is as the heads of serpents which the disbelievers shall eat from. In his Reference (2112), he says: That the Arabs apply the name Shaitan to a sort of serpent having a mane, ugly or foul in the head and face. In Mr. Abdullah Usuf Ali's translation of the Holy Qur-an in English, in the same chapter and verse (37:65), it reads: The shoots of its fruit stalks are like the heads of devils.

The Bible's forbidden tree (Gen. 2:17) was a tree of the knowledge of good and evil. This also tells us that the tree was a person, for trees know nothing! This tree of knowledge was forbidden to Adam and Eve. The only one whom this tree could be is the devil. After deceiving Adam and his wife, he has been called a serpent due to his keen knowledge of tricks and his acts of shrewdness; he made his acquaintance with Adam and his wife in the absence of God. Since this is the nature of a liar, he can best lie to the people when truth is absent.

We know that there was never a time when an actual serpent (or snake) could talk and deceive people in the knowledge of God's law. This same serpent is mentioned in Revelation 12:9 as a deceiver. There (12:9) it is made clear to us that the serpent is The dragon, devil and satan which deceiveth the whole world. In Gen. (3:1) he appeared in the Garden of Paradise before the woman and deceived her (Rev. 12:4). He stood before the woman who was ready to be delivered to devour her child as soon as it is born.

The serpent, the devil, dragon, satan, seems to have been seeking the weaker part of man (the woman) to bring to naught the man -- the Divine Man. It is his first and last trick to deceive the people of God through the woman or with the woman. He is using his woman to tempt the black man by parading her half-nude before his eyes and with public love-making, indecent kissing and dancing over radio and television screens and throughout their public papers and magazines. He is flooding the world with propaganda against God and His true religion, Islam. He stands before the so-called Negro woman to deceive her by feigning love and love-making with her, give the so-called Negro woman preference over her husband or brother in hiring.

In some cities, the Negro woman receives a much higher salary than the so-called Negro man. The devil takes the so-called Negro woman and puts his hands and arms around her body. She may be married or single, it makes no difference. Whenever he can he is making eyes at her. This is an outright destruction of the moral principles of the black man.

In some cities, we convert five to one woman. The so-called Negroes should unite and put a stop to the destruction of their women by the serpent. The woman in (Rev. 12:4) actually refers to the last Apostle of God, and her child refers to his followers, or the entire Negro race as they are called, who are not ready to be delivered (go to their own). **Pgs. 126-127 MTBM**

Reference 36: Devils Seek To Slay The Negroes

Psalms 37:32

"The wicked lie in wait for the righteous, intent on putting them to death."

    Allah (God) has found His people (the so-called Negroes), and is angry with the slave-masters for the evil done by them to His people (the so-called Negroes). Allah (God) is going to repay them according to their doings.

    My poor people who have turned to their own God and religion (Allah and Islam), are being tracked down and watched as though they are about to rob a bank. This is done to try and put fear in them -- so that they might stay away from their God (Allah) and His true religion (Islam), as the devil knows -- their salvation and defense.

    They (the devils) watch the steps of the righteous (the Negroes) and seek to slay them (Psalms 37:32). The so-called Negroes live under the very shadow of death in America. There is no justice for them in the courts of their slave-masters. Why should not America be chastised for her evils done to the so-called Negroes? If God destroyed ancient Babylon for the mockery made of the sacred vessels taken from the Temple in Jerusalem, what do you think Allah (God) should do for America's mockery of the so-called Negroes -- that she took from their native land and people and filled them with wine and whiskey.

Now she (America) puts on a show of temptation with their women (white women) in newspapers, magazines, in the streets half nude, and posing in the so-called Negroes' faces in the most indecent manner that is known to mankind -- to trick them (so-called Negroes) to death and hell along with them. Be wise, my people, and shut our eyes to them -- do not look at them in such an indecent way. Clean your homes of white people's pictures -- put your own on the walls. The only so-called Negroes' pictures you will see in their homes are the one they have lynched, one they want to kill, or one who has betrayed his own people for them.

America is falling; she is a habitation of devils and every uncleanness and hateful people of the righteous. Forsake her and fly to your own before it is too late. Pgs. 274-275 MTBM

References 37 & 38:
Don't Try To Master Heaven And Earth

Isaiah 14:13

"You said in your heart, 'I will ascend to the heavens; I will raise my throne above the stars of God; I will sit enthroned on the mount of assembly, on the utmost heights of Mount Zaphon.'"

Isaiah 14:16

"Those who see you stare at you, they ponder your fate: 'Is this the man who shook the earth and made kingdoms tremble?'"

Man is easily made, but the sun, moon and stars are much harder to make. Yet we are the makers of them. In making the moon, it was not our original father's intention to make the moon as it is. His real intention was to destroy the moon (earth) but failed and all others who make such attempts will fail.

What! You disbelieve it? Do you not see that the devils are trying to make themselves a satellite to make you believe that they are the masters of the heavens and earth, as it is written of them in the Bible and Holy Qur-an (Isaiah 14:13, 14-16th verses).

They destroyed other people, cities and opened not the house of his prisoners. None has fulfilled this prophecy better than America. She has destroyed other nations' cities while she has not suffered the loss of one of her cities by a foreign nation, while preaching the freedom of her own people from the powers of other nations.

She holds a whole nation (so-called Negroes) prisoner, and refuses to open the door of freedom, justice and equality to them. She threatens to go to war against other nations who hold any of her citizens prisoners. They now boast of building rockets to land on our moon (which can't and won't be done); and to build a small contraption to try circling the earth like our moon, which we have made to revolve around the earth.

The following is from the Holy Qur-an: And we (the devils) sought to reach heaven, but we found it filled with strong guards and flames; and we (the devils) used to sit in some of the sitting-places thereof to steal a hearing. But he who tries to listen now finds a flame lying in wait for him (Holy Qur-an 72:8,9).

I am for the separation of my people from their enemies; that they share not in the enemies' destruction, even though I may lose my own life in this daring attempt to save them by the plain, simple truth of God and power. It must be done and will be done, regardless of whom or what. It can be done in one day, but Allah desires to make Himself known in the West, as it is written of Him.

Pgs. 109-110 MTBM

"How have these insights impacted you so far? Share your reflections and connect with like-minded believers in our growing community on Facebook. Your voice and perspective matter."

 https://www.facebook.com/TheNewWorldNationOfIslam

Reference 39: Enemy Sentenced to Death

Revelation 20:10-14

"And the devil, who deceived them, was thrown into the lake of burning sulfur, where the beast and the false prophet had been thrown. They will be tormented day and night for ever and ever."

Revelation 20:11

"Then I saw a great white throne and him who was seated on it. The earth and the heavens fled from his presence, and there was no place for them."

Revelation 20:12

"And I saw the dead, great and small, standing before the throne, and books were opened. Another book was opened, which is the book of life. The dead were judged according to what they had done as recorded in the books."

Revelation 20:13

"The sea gave up the dead that were in it, and death and Hades gave up the dead that were in them, and each person was judged according to what they had done."

Revelation 20:14

"Then death and Hades were thrown into the lake of fire. The lake of fire is the second death."

We hear the statement of black educational, political and Christian classes, which express their love for the white man, publicly asking to be his brothers, if not his brothers-in-law. Now, this class wants to make it clear to the world that they really love the white race and not the black race. This means they want to be white instead of black. The devils have made them hate black. They reject the thought of black ever being the ruler or equal with the ruler. They ask boldly for inferiority, not only for themselves, but for their people.

They want to absorb themselves and their kind (especially the so-called American Negro) into the race of white people, thus ending the black race. It is just the opposite with Allah (God), myself and my followers. We "want out completely." We want no claim to kinship with a people who, by nature, are not our kin. Read from Genesis to the Revelation in the Bible and from Sura 2 to Sura 114 of the Holy Qur-an.

By no means are the so-called Negroes and the whites kin. God did not create them to ever become brothers. One is created an enemy against the other, and since the righteous are more powerful than the wicked, Allah, the God of righteous, set a time of reckoning for the enemy (the white man) of the righteous.

We want separation. We want a home on this earth we can call our own. We want to go for self and leave the enemy who has been sentenced to death by Allah (Rev. 20:10-14) from the day he was created (See this subject in the Bible and Qur-an). No one, white, black, brown, yellow or red can prove to me by any scriptures of Allah (God) sent by one of the prophets of Allah

(God) that we should not be separated from the white race, that we should believe and follow the religion dictated, shaped and formed by the theologians of the white race. **Pgs. 271-272 MTBM**

Reference 41: Every Heart Shall Melt

Ezekiel 21:7

"And when they ask you, 'Why are you groaning?' you shall say, 'Because of the news that is coming. Every heart will melt with fear and every hand go limp; every spirit will become faint and every leg will be weak as water.' It is coming! It will surely take place, declares the Sovereign Lord."

Reference 42: Fall Of America

Revelation 18:2

"With a mighty voice he shouted: 'Fallen! Fallen is Babylon the Great! She has become a dwelling for demons and a haunt for every impure spirit, a haunt for every unclean bird, a haunt for every unclean and detestable animal.'"

Revelation 18:4

"Then I heard another voice from heaven say: 'Come out of her, my people, so that you will not share in her sins, so that you will not receive any of her plagues.'"

Revelation 18:5

"For her sins are piled up to heaven, and God has remembered her crimes."

THE DECLINE OF THE DOLLAR
(Chapter from MTBM By The Honorable Mr. Elijah Muhammad)

The stronghold of the American Government is falling to pieces. She has lost her prestige among the nations of the earth. One of the greatest powers of America was her dollar. The loss of such power will bring any nation to weakness, for this is the media of exchange between nations. The English pound and the American dollar have been the power and beckoning light of these two great powers. But when the world went off the gold and silver standard, the financial doom of England and America was sealed.

The pound has lost 50 per cent of its value. America's dollar has lost everything now as power backing for her currency, which was once backed by gold for every $5.00 note and up. All of her currency was backed by silver from a $1.00 note and up.

Today, the currency of America is not backed by any sound value, silver or gold. The note today is something that the government declares it will give you the value in return but does not name that value. They definitely are not backing their currency with silver or gold.

This is the number one fall, and it is very clear that the loss of the power of the American dollar means the loss of the financial power of America. What will happen, since there is no sound backing for her notes, we do not know.

What should we expect even in the next 12 months under the fall of the power of America's dollar? This means that we have 100 per cent inflation. What could happen under 100 per cent inflation? Your guess is as good as mine. The power of gold and silver was once abundant in America. But the touch of the finger of

God against the power of so mighty a nation has now caused the crumbling and fall of America.

We can easily and truthfully liken the fall of America to the prophetic symbolic picture given in the (Bible) Revelation of John (18:2). The name Babylon used there does not really say whether it is ancient Babylon or a picture of some future Babylon.

The description it gives is as follows: *"And he [angel] cried mightily with a strong voice [with authority] saying, Babylon the great is fallen, is fallen and is become the habitation of devils [Allah has declared the people to be a race of devils], and the hole of every foul spirit and a cage of every unclean and hateful bird."* The description here given to the Babylon by the Prophets compares with the present history and people of America and their fall.

The picture shows the cause of her fall. First, she had become the habitation of devils, making her a haven for every people that love the works and doings of the devil. Here the Prophet refers to them symbolically, as being a hole of every foul spirit and a cage of every unclean and hateful bird.

People are referred to as birds, snakes, beasts, fish and other animals to tell or represent the characteristics of that person. It is universally known that the very beginning of the American people was from the lower class of European people. Their first ruler (President Washington) was a fugitive from England. The common, dissatisfied and lower grade of European people followed and boosted his authority. This filled and inhabited America with a very low-class and low-based people.

Then this type of people went into Africa and purchased slaves from among our people, who were also uneducated, most of them, but there were a few who were highly educated. All of these begin to mix with the low-based, evil-minded, real citizens of the Western Hemisphere (whites). When America began to get strong in power, she opened her doors to the underprivileged (laborers) in overpopulated countries, such as China, Japan and other European states, to seek citizenship in America.

This brought America into being one of the most mixed people who were granted the freedom to live any kind of life they chose. They were not forced to serve the God of the Universe who made heaven and earth, or any religion. They had freedom to worship. This made America a haven for any people who wished to be free of the compelling aspects of religious and just rule and authority. This people for the past 500 years has put into practice every evil that is imaginable.

The freedom of uncleanliness is granted and is worshiped. The percentage of sexual worship of the same sex is greater than in any other government on the face of the earth. Little children are being taught sex almost from the cradle, making the whole nation, as one man put it, nearly 90 per cent freaks of nature.

On the streets of any metropolitan city in America, it is common to see men sweethearting with men and women sweethearting with women. Little boys with boys and little girls with girls.

It is so common that a decent family is puzzled as to where to send their children for schooling. There are no all-girl schools as there once were. They are all-girl schools of sweethearts. The same sex falling upon their own. Boys' colleges are breeding such filthy practices, the jails, prisons, and the Federal Penitentiaries are all breeding dens of homosexuals.

As the Prophet says in the 18th chapter: "She is a cage of every unclean and hateful bird." There are types of hateful birds. This is why a symbolic name is given. It means human beings. There are birds of prey and birds that are unclean, such as crows, owls, buzzards and ravens, who live and thrive off the carcasses of others. And there are unclean people living and thriving off the unclean.

It is time that God intervenes to bring about an end of such people as the wicked of America. She offers the same filth to all of the civilized people of the earth, and she hates you if you are against her way of life and will threaten you with death as the Sodomites did Lot and his followers. But I say to you, as the 4th verse of Chapter 18 says: You that want to be a better people than this, "come out of her."

The so-called American Negroes are referred to here in the 4th verse as being God's people (My People): "Come out of her that ye be not partakers of her sins and that you receive not of her plagues."

This is a call to the American so-called Negroes to give up a doomed, wicked people that have destroyed them from being a people worthy of recognition and who have now become lovers of their enemies and destroyers.

The 5th verse tells us that "Her sins have reached into heaven and God has remembered her iniquities and is ready to destroy her." Her destruction cometh quickly according to the 8th verse, that plagues of death, mourning and famines which cometh in one day (one year) and then after that she shall be destroyed by fire, utterly burned.

This is backed up in these words: "Strong is the Lord God who judge her." Here it gives us a knowledge that He who judges is well able with power, with wisdom and with deliberate and careful maneuvering to give judgment against her. **Pgs. 275-278 MTBM**

This guide is only the beginning. For those who wish to absorb these teachings more deeply, an **audiobook version of Guide to Understanding the Bible** is available. Listen anytime, anywhere, and let the wisdom unfold with you on the go.

 https://nwnoimedia.com/thankyou-page-2123

Reference 43: Fear God Who Has Power

Revelation 21:8

"But the cowardly, the unbelieving, the vile, the murderers, the sexually immoral, those who practice magic arts, the idolaters and all liars—they will be consigned to the fiery lake of burning sulfur. This is the second death."

Reference 44: Fear Of Man

Proverbs 29:25

"Fear of man will prove to be a snare, but whoever trusts in the Lord is kept safe."

Fear is the number one enemy that is blocking progress and success from coming to the so-called Negroes of America. This fear causes them to grieve. The whole world knows the poor so-called Negroes of America have suffered and still suffer more grief and sorrow than any people on the earth! This fear is the fear of a slave-masters (white man) and what the slave-masters dislike. Let the so-called Negroes submit to Allah (God) and they will not fear anymore, nor will they grieve. As it is written: "The fear of man bringeth a snare." (Proverbs: 29:25). It has surely snared the so-called Negroes.

The Lord of the world's Finder of we the loss members of the Asiatic Black Nation for 400 years said that the slave-masters put fear in our Fathers when they were babies. Allah is the only one that can remove this fear from us, but he will not remove it from us until we submit to His will, not our will, and fear Him and Him alone. Then, as it is written, "And it shall come to pass in the day that the Lord shall give thee rest from sorrow and from thy fear, and from the hard bondage wherein thou wast made to serve."(Isaiah 14:3). There are so many places that I could point out in the Bible and Holy Qur-an that warn us of fearing our enemies above or equal to the fear of Allah (God). It is a fool who has greater fear of the devils (white man) than Allah who has the power to destroy the devils and their followers (Revelation 21:8; Holy Qur-an 7:18 and 15:43). **Pgs. 29-30 MTBM**

Reference 45: Fearful And Unbelieving

Revelation 21:8

"But the cowardly, the unbelieving, the vile, the murderers, the sexually immoral, those who practice magic arts, the idolaters and all liars—they will be consigned to the fiery lake of burning sulfur. This is the second death."

The Truth must triumph over falsehood, as day triumphs over night. When we deny the truth it shows that we love falsehood more than truth. If we fear to speak the truth for the sake of falsehood, this is not only hiding the truth, but is actually showing fear and distrust in the Divine Supreme Being, His wisdom and His power.

This hiding and mixing the truth with falsehood because of fear of the enemy (devils) is taking a great number of our people to hell with the devils.

It is natural for one to fear that of which he has no knowledge. However, when Truth and Knowledge are made clear to you, you have no cloak for your fear. Your mixing up Truth with falsehood is only because you fear your enemy (the devils).

Allah (God) doesn't care for us when our fear is greater for our enemies than for Him. Allah says: I and I alone, should you fear. Believe in that which I have revealed, verifying that which is with you, and be not the first to deny it; neither take a mean price for my message; and keep your duty to Me, and to Me alone (Holy Qur-an 2:40-41).

Once the so-called Negroes drop slavery (Christianity), and accept Allah for their God, and His religion (Islam) Allah will remove their fear and grief, and they will not fear nor grieve any more.

It is a shame to see our people in such fearful condition. The fearful and the unbelieving shall have their part in the lake which burns with fire and brimstone which is the second death (Rev. 21:8).

The devil whom they fear more than Allah (God) was not able to protect himself against Allah; therefore his followers shared with him the fire of hell. They had suffered one death (mental), and by fearing the devils and rejecting the truth, they suffered a physical death, which was the final death. **Pg. 99 MTBM**

Reference 46: Fed And Sheltered Israel In Desert

Exodus 16:12

"I have heard the grumbling of the Israelites. Tell them, 'At twilight you will eat meat, and in the morning you will be filled with bread. Then you will know that I am the Lord your God.'"

Exodus 16:13

"That evening quail came and covered the camp, and in the morning there was a layer of dew around the camp."

Exodus 16:14

"When the dew was gone, thin flakes like frost on the ground appeared on the desert floor."

Exodus 16:15

"When the Israelites saw it, they said to each other, 'What is it?' For they did not know what it was. Moses said to them, 'It is the bread the Lord has given you to eat.'"

The time has arrived, and you must know the truth of this race and yourself and nation. You must be reunited to your own Nation. The time is ripe for your return. You will never again be slaves to any other nation. Allah will make you the head and not the tail. Accept your own! Stop destroying yourself trying to be other than your own kind and patterning after a doomed race of devils. You may say, How am I to live without going along with my enemies desires? They did not create themselves -- we are their creators -- our father, the Black man, feeds them. Is it not our God who created food for all?

He raises the clouds from the earth and causes them to pour their water on the thirsty parts and causes the seeds to germinate and grow for your food. Can this devil whom you trust do these things? And is it not Allah (God) who has made the earth to rotate on her axis in such a way that she causes changes in seasons four times a year to satisfy life and vegetation in all parts of the earth.

You are letting the devils fool and disgrace you and are taking you to hell with them! Your God, Allah, will be happy and will rejoice in feeding, clothing and sheltering you if you believe. The Bible teaches you that He fed and sheltered Israel in the desert (Exod. 16:12-15). Fear not, Allah (God) is with us. The enemies of Allah and the righteous are leading you only to evil and indecency, as the Holy Qur-an teaches you and me.

They are pulling off your clothes and showing the world your shame, and you think it is right. They are used to going nude. They have nudist colonies here in America to prove it. Four thousand years ago all of Europe was a nudist colony. And your little daughters are being brought up to not be shy of indecency.

You have them stripped to their trunks, all because the devils invited you to wear such styles of theirs, and you are obeying. This is to tempt the black people in becoming sharers in their doom.

Your common sense teaches you that God does not approve of such filth. This should also bring you into the knowledge that the religion (Christianity) so talked and preached of by the white race is only a bit for you to swallow to become the followers of them (the enemies of God). Your loving and sweethearting them only means that you are in love with the devils in person, and you are courting death and hell fire. Believe this or leave it. Read Holy Qur-an 7:27, O children of Adam, let not the devil seduce you, as he expelled your parents from the garden (this was done by the father of this race, Yakub, 6,000 years ago) pulling off from their clothing that he might show them their shame, he surely sees you as his host.

They make fools of you and then laugh at you for being dumb enough for them to trick. (The devil scientists and rulers prepare the trap for you and the others spring it on you.) The above verse you are now fulfilling by going partly nude. You have confidence in the devils because you do not know them to be devils. You are now being taught, and there will be no excuse for your taking them for friends instead of Allah. **Pgs. 100-101 MTBM**

Reference 47: First Parents Of White Race

Genesis 3:20

"Adam named his wife Eve, because she would become the mother of all the living."

Genesis 3:21

"The Lord God made garments of skin for Adam and his wife and clothed them."

Genesis 3:22

"And the Lord God said, 'The man has now become like one of us, knowing good and evil. He must not be allowed to reach out his hand and take also from the tree of life and eat, and live forever.'"

Genesis 3:23

"So the Lord God banished him from the Garden of Eden to work the ground from which he had been taken."

Genesis 3:24

"After he drove the man out, he placed on the east side of the Garden of Eden cherubim and a flaming sword flashing back and forth to guard the way to the tree of life."

THE WHITE RACE'S FALSE CLAIM TO BE DIVINE, CHOSEN PEOPLE
(Chapter from MTBM By The Honorable Mr. Elijah Muhammad)

According to the Bible (Gen. 3:20-24), Adam and his wife were the first parents of all people (white race only) and the first sinners. According to the Word of Allah, he was driven from the Garden of Paradise into the hills and caves of West Asia, or as they now call it, "Europe," to live his evil life in the West and not in the Holy Land of the East. "Therefore, the Lord God sent him (Adam) forth from the Garden of Eden, to till the ground from when he was taken. So He drove out the man; and He placed at the east of the Garden of Eden cherubims (Muslim guards) and a flaming sword which turned every way to keep the devils out of the way of the tree of life (the nation of Islam)." The sword of Islam prevented the Adamic race from crossing the border of Europe and Asia to make trouble among the Muslims for 2,000 years after they were driven out of the Holy Land and away from the people, for their mischief-making, lying and disturbing the peace of the righteous nation of Islam.

The Holy Qur-an says: "But the devil made them both fall from it, and caused them to depart from that (state) in which they were; and we said: Get forth, some of you being the enemies of others, and there is for you in the earth an abode and a provision for a time!" (The time here refers to the limited time of the Adamic race. The time is 6,000 years.) According to the above verse

(2:36), they were driven out because they were the enemies of the people of the Garden, in these words: "Get forth some of you being the enemies of others." The others cannot refer to any others than the people of the Garden (the Muslims).

The Adamic race is still the enemy of the Muslims (the black man). Nevertheless, Allah did not deprive the Adamic race right guidance through His prophets, whom they persecuted and killed. The Adamic white race's history is proof that they are the enemies of God and the righteous, for they never did sincerely accept a prophet of God. Can they now claim to be the chosen race of God? Why would God limit their time of rule? Why did God send His prophets to warn them that He was going to destroy them? Holy Qur-an (7:14): "He said (the devil) respite me until the day when they are raised up." Those that are referred to as being "raised up" refer to the resurrection of the black man into the knowledge of the white race as being the devils, the enemies of Allah (God) and the black nation. "He as (the devil) said: "Thou hast caused me to remain disappointed, I will certainly lie in wait for them in Thy straight path" (Holy Qur-an 7:166). What Allah disappointed the devils in was the limiting of their rule over the nations and making it manifest to the world of black man that they are the enemies and great deceivers of the righteous.

The white race is not, and never will be, the chosen people of Allah (God). They are the chosen people of their father Yakub, the devil. **Pgs. 133-134 MTBM**

"The journey to understanding is not meant to be traveled alone. Our community welcomes those who seek knowledge and are ready to engage in meaningful discussions about these teachings. Join us and connect with others who are committed to the truth."

📌 https://nwnoicommunity.aitribes.app/ft/axkVr)

Reference 48: Flesh And Blood Cannot Enter Heaven

1 Corinthians 15:50

"I declare to you, brothers and sisters, that flesh and blood cannot inherit the kingdom of God, nor does the perishable inherit the imperishable."

The prophets teach us to let the past judgments of people, their cities, and their warner's serve as a lesson, or sign of the last judgment and its warner's. Noah did not know the hour of the flood. Lot did not know the Hour of Sodom and Gomorrah until the Executors had arrived, and Jesus prophesied; (Matt.24:37-39), "it will be the same in the last judgment of the world of Satan." You have gone astray because of your misunderstanding of the scripture, the Prophet Jesus, and the coming of God to judge the world. My corrections are not accepted.

Your misunderstanding and misinterpretation of it is really the joy of devils. For it is the devils' desire to keep the so-called Negroes ignorant of the truth of God until they see it with their eyes. The truth of God is the salvation and freedom of the so called Negroes from the devils' power.

Can you blame them? No! Blame yourself for being so foolish as to allow the devils to fool you in not accepting the truth after it comes to you. The devils have tried to deceive the people all over the earth with Christianity, that is, God the Father, Jesus the Son, the Holy Ghost; three Gods into One God. The resurrection of the Son and His return to judge the world; or that the Son is in some place above the earth, sitting on the right-hand side of the Father, waiting until the Father makes His enemies His footstool. The period of waiting is 2,000 years. Yet, He died for the Father to save His enemies (the whole world of sinners).

My friends, use a bit of common sense. First, could a wonderful flesh and blood body, made of the essence of our earth, last 2,000 years on the earth, or off the earth, without being healed! Second, where exists such a heaven, of the earth, that flesh and blood of the earth can exist, since the Bible teaches that flesh and blood cannot enter heaven? (Cor. 15:50)

Flesh and blood cannot survive without that of which it is made, the earth. Jesus' prophesy of the coming of the Son of Man is very clear, if you rightly understand. First, this removes all doubt about who we should expect to execute judgment, for if man is to be judged and rewarded according to his actions, who could be justified in sitting as judge of man's doings but another man? How could a spirit be our judge when we cannot see a spirit? And ever since life was created, life has had spirit. But the Bible teaches that God will be seen on the Day of Judgment. Not only the righteous will see Him, but even His enemies shall see Him. **Pgs. 10-12 MTBM**

Reference 49: Garden Of Paradise

Genesis 3:1

"Now the serpent was more crafty than any of the wild animals the Lord God had made. He said to the woman, 'Did God really say, "You must not eat from any tree in the garden"?'"

The Bible's forbidden tree (Gen. 2:17) was a tree of the knowledge of good and evil. This also tells us that the tree was person, for trees know nothing! This tree of knowledge was forbidden to Adam and Eve. The only one whom this tree could be is the devil. After deceiving Adam and his wife, he has been called a serpent due to his keen knowledge of tricks and his acts of shrewdness; he made his acquaintance with Adam and his wife in the absence of God. Since this is the nature of a liar, he can best lie to the people when truth is absent.

We know that there was never a time when an actual serpent (or snake) could talk and deceive people in the knowledge of God's law. This same serpent is mentioned in Revelation 12:9 as a deceiver. There (12:9) it is made clear to us that the serpent is The dragon, devil and satan which deceiveth the whole world. In Gen. (3:1) he appeared in the Garden of Paradise before the woman and deceived her (Rev. 12:4). He stood before the woman who was ready to be delivered to devour her child as soon as it is born.

The serpent, the devil, dragon, satan, seems to have been seeking the weaker part of man (the woman) to bring to naught the man -- the Divine Man. It is his first and last trick to deceive the people of God through the woman or with the woman. He is using his woman to tempt the black man by parading her half-nude before his eyes and with public love-making, indecent kissing and dancing over radio and television screens and throughout their public papers and magazines. He is flooding the world with propaganda against God and His true religion, Islam. He stands before the so-called Negro woman to deceive her by feigning love and love-making with her, give the so-called Negro woman preference over her husband or brother in hiring.

In some cities, the Negro woman receives as much higher salary than the so-called Negro man. The devil takes the so-called Negro woman and puts his hands and arms around her body. She may be married or single, it makes no difference. Whenever he can he is making eyes at her. This is an outright destruction of the moral principles of the black man.

In some cities, we convert five to one woman. The so-called Negroes should unite and put a stop to the destruction of their women by the serpent. The woman in (Rev. 12:4) actually refers to the last Apostle of God, and her child refers to his followers, or the entire Negro race as they are called, who are not ready to be delivered (go to their own). **Pgs. 126-127 MTBM**

Reference 50: Gentiles Prepare War

Joel 3:9

"Proclaim this among the nations: Prepare for war! Rouse the warriors! Let all the fighting men draw near and attack."

It is clear that the armies of the nations of the earth have geared themselves for a showdown between their forces and Allah and the Nation of Islam. We, the so-called American Negroes, the lost and found members of our Nation, are in this decision. The second and third verses of this same chapter (Chapter 3) read like this: "I will also gather all nations and will bring them down into the valley of Jehoshaphat [Europe and Asia -- between black and white] and will please with them there for my people and for my heritage [the lost and found, so-called Negroes], Israel whom they have scattered among the nations and parted by land [between the European white race] and they have casted lots for my people and have given a boy for a harlot and sold a girl for wine that they might drink" (Joel 3:2, 3).

American has fulfilled this to the very letter and spirit with her slaves (the so-called Negroes) under the type of Israel. The Egyptians did nothing of the kind of Israel when they were in bondage to them. In fact, and as God taught me, the Bible is not referring to those people as His People, it is referring to the so-called Negro and his enemy (the white race). The seventh verse also gives us a hint in this way:

"Behold, I will raise them out of the place where you have sold them and will return our recompence upon your own head" (Joel 3:7).

The slave-masters of our fathers must reap what they have sown. Allah calls them to war in the ninth verse of the same chapter.

"Proclaim you among the Gentiles, prepare war, wake up the mighty men, let all of the men of war draw near, let them come up" (Joel 3:9).

All the mighty men of science and modern warfare have been called in an effort to devise instruments and weapons against God and the armies of heaven. The nations of the earth are angry. The disbelievers and hypocrites of my people also are angry over the change of the old world to a new world of justice and righteousness, causing much spiritual darkness and misunderstanding to fall upon them. They want to judge the person Allah should choose for His Messenger. **Pgs. 268-269 MTBM**

Reference 51: God Pleads With You To Get Out Of America

Revelation 18:4

"Then I heard another voice from heaven say: 'Come out of her, my people, so that you will not share in her sins, so that you will not receive any of her plagues.'"

The coming Allah and the judgement of the wicked world is made clear by the prophetic sayings of the Prophets. The so-called reverends and the proud intellectual class are doomed to destruction with the enemy, if they remain with him instead of joining onto Allah, Who loves them and Who will deliver them and the Nation of Islam.

The so-called Negro masses must be warned of the grave mistake they make in following the leadership of those who love and befriend their murderers. This will not get them freedom or civil rights.

America is falling. Her doom has come, and none said the prophets shall help her in the day of her downfall. In the Bible, God pleads with you to fly out of her (America) and seek refuge in Him (Rev. 18:4). What is going to happen in 1965 and 1966? It certainly will change your minds about following a doomed people, a people who hate you and your kind and who call one who teaches the truth about them a hater. They are the producers of hatred of us. We are with God and the righteous. **Pgs. 272-273 MTBM**

Reference 52: God's Power

Habakkuk 3:4

"His splendor was like the sunrise; rays flashed from his hand, where his power was hidden."

According to the dictionary of the Bible: Teman, a son of Esau by Adah (Gen. 36:11, 15, 42) and in I Chron. 1:36, now if Habakkuk saw God come or coming from the sons of Esau (Eliphaz), then God must be a man and not a spook. If Habakkuk's (3:3) prophecy refers to some country, town, or city, if there be any truth at all in this prophecy, then we can say that this prophet saw God as a material being, belonging to the human family of the earth-and not to a spirit (ghost).

In the same chapter and verse, Habakkuk saw the Holy One from Mount Paran. This is also earthly, somewhere in Arabia.

Here the Bible makes a difference between God and another person who is called the Holy One. Which one should we take for our God? For one is called God, while another One is called Holy One. The Holy One: His glory covered the heavens and the earth was full of His praise. It has been a long time since the earth was full of praise for a Holy One. Even to this hour, the people do not care for Holy People and will persecute and kill the Holy One, if God does not intervene.

In the fourth verse of the above chapter, it says, "He had horns coming out of his hands: and there was the hiding of His power." Such science to represent the God's power could confuse the ignorant masses of the world. Two gods are here represented at the same time. (It is good that God makes Himself manifest to the ignorant world today.) **Pg. 7 MTBM**

Reference 53: Great Deceiver

Revelation 20:3

"He threw him into the Abyss, and locked and sealed it over him, to keep him from deceiving the nations anymore until the thousand years were ended. After that, he must be set free for a short time."

Revelation 20:4

"I saw thrones on which were seated those who had been given authority to judge. And I saw the souls of those who had been beheaded because of their testimony about Jesus and because of the word of God. They had not worshiped the beast or its image and had not received its mark on their foreheads or their hands. They came to life and reigned with Christ a thousand years."

Revelation 20:5

"(The rest of the dead did not come to life until the thousand years were ended.) This is the first resurrection."

Revelation 20:6

"Blessed and holy are those who share in the first resurrection. The second death has no power over them, but they will be priests of God and of Christ and will reign with him for a thousand years."

Revelation 20:7

"When the thousand years are over, Satan will be released from his prison."

Revelation 20:8

"And will go out to deceive the nations in the four corners of the earth—Gog and Magog—and to gather them for battle. In number they are like the sand on the seashore."

A religion used by the devils to convert people cannot be accepted by Allah, especially when it did not come from Him.

We all know that Christianity is from the white race. Should we be surprised at this late day to see it come to pass? Think over the saying of your own Bible. "The great deceiver of the nations?" (Rev. 20:3-8). Of course, he deceived them (the so-called Negroes) that had received his mark (the mark of Christianity, the cross).

More than anyone else, those who worship his image (the so-called Negroes) are guilty of loving the white race and all that race stands for. One can even find the pictures of white people on the walls, mantel, shelves, dressers and tables of their homes.

Some carry them on their person. The so-called Negroes go to church and bow down to their statues under the name of Jesus and Mary and some under the name of Jesus' disciples, which are only the images of the white race, their arch-deceiver.

They even worship the white race's names, which will not exist among the people of the new world, for they are not the names of God.

The so-called Negroes would greatly benefit themselves if they would seek their places in "that" which Allah (God) makes new by giving back to the great deceiver his religion (Christianity), churches and names and accept the religion of their righteous nation, Islam, a name of their God, which is unlimited in the eyes of any white person. **Pg. 83 MTBM**

Reference 54: He Departed From Evil Maketh Himself A Prey

Isaiah 59:15

"Truth is nowhere to be found, and whoever shuns evil becomes a prey. The Lord looked and was displeased that there was no justice."

REPLY TO A JUDGE
(Chapter from MTBM By The Honorable Mr. Elijah Muhammad)

On November 8, 1963, according to the Chicago Tribune newspaper, Federal Judge F. Ryan Duffy ruled that the Black Muslim "sect" is not a religion but is rather racist and has for its objective the overthrow of the white race. He further charged the believers of Islam inside prison walls as having a impressive history of inciting riots and violence.

I asked Judge Duffy to prove his charges. This is not true. In 1943, I was sent to the Federal Penitentiary in Milan, Michigan, for nothing other than to be kept out of the public and from teaching my people the truth during the war between America, Germany, and Japan. This war came to a halt in 1945 when America dropped an atomic bomb on Japan. And the following year, in August, 1946, I was released on what the institution called "good time" for being a model prisoner who was obedient to the prison rules and laws.

In the year 1942-43, according to reports, there were nearly a hundred of my followers sentenced to prison terms of from 1 to 5 years for refusing to take part in the war between America, Japan and Germany because of our peaceful stand and the principle belief and practice in Islam, which is peace.

The very dominant idea in Islam is the making of peace and not war; our refusing to go armed is our proof that we want peace. We felt that we had no right to take part in a war with nonbelievers of Islam who have always denied us justice and equal rights; and if we were going to be examples of peace and righteousness (as Allah has chosen us to be), we felt we had no right to join hands with the murderers of people or to help murder those who have done us no wrong. What would justify such actions? Let the truth answer.

Judge Duffy listened to an appeal made by a new convert to Islam who is serving a 200-year sentence, charged with slaying two Chicago men in 1951. (He should be given credit for his desire to be a Muslim). The appeal was asking for the freedom of obtaining publications and reading material distributed by the Black Muslims, including the Holy Qur-an.

According to the rules and laws of the prison -- before we Muslims began to be imprisoned -- all religious believers, regardless to their religion and God, were permitted access to their books and visits by their religious teachers. This freedom is written in the Constitution for everyone, but when we were imprisoned that freedom was denied us and us alone. And this is the freedom that is guaranteed in the American Constitution. A person is free to criticize anyone he wants, even if it is the Congress or President of the United States of America.

But while the Constitution of America was being written, our fathers were slaves, and we, today, are merely free slaves who do not have the knowledge of self and have not registered with Allah and His religion, the Nation of Islam.

When I was admitted into Cook County jail in Chicago, I wanted the Holy Qur-an, too, but I was denied having it, though it is not a "sect's Bible." It is the religious scriptures and guide for the Muslim world, recognized universally as the last revelation given to the world. And the Holy Qur-an has been the Holy book and scripture for all Muslims for the past 1,381 years.

We are not an organization; we are a world. I use the same Holy Qur-an that all Muslims use; the book that is universally recognized as being 100 per cent true. And such scholar and U.S. Judge as F. Ryan Duffy calls it a "sect's book."

One of the officers, who was a very fine man, tried in vain to persuade the warden in the Cook County jail to allow me to have my Holy Qur-an as other religious believers were receiving theirs in prison. But this same officer came back and told me that the warden said "That is what we put them in prison for, and to let us read the Bible, ha, ha, ha."

They do not even want to hear the truth of the Bible; for there is no paradise in it for them. According to their own Bible that they wish all black people to read, when carefully understood, Genesis to Revelation teaches that they were an appointed people for hell fire from the beginning of their creation. I am ready to prove this with any scholar or scientist. They hated Judge Rutherford for his interpretation of the Bible which condemned the church and its father, the Pope of Rome.

The Chicago Tribune also quoted Judge Duffy as saying that a social study showed that the Black Muslim movement, despite its pretext of a religious facade, is an organization that has for its objective the overthrow of the white race. But when have the so-called Negroes in America been classified as social members in the white American society; even in Christianity, not to think of social equality and human relationship?

The so-called Negroes have never been equally recognized members in anything in America as far as the white man is concerned. Nor even in their prisons are they recognized equally with the white race.

How can he or anyone put us under social study when there is no social equality between whites and so-called Negroes? This gradually brewing revolution is to reclaim our respect as human beings and equal members in the civilized society of the nations of earth. Isn't it true that this is what the fight going on in the South today is for; where poor, so-called Negroes are being beaten, shot down and bombed in even those churches that the white man permits them to have because they want to be recognized as equal members in the society or order of the American white people?

We have turned to our God, Allah, and His religion, Islam, and our own people, where there is no such thing as distinction. We want to be separated from our open enemies, the slave-masters' children, who desire nothing more than to mistreat us.

When have we, the Muslims, ever received justice under the Constitution of America? Not one time in the courts of America, a country and people that hate the religion of Islam because it demands freedom, justice and equality for black people.

The greatest racists that have ever lived on our Planet Earth are the white people. We only ask for the privilege of being ourselves, seeking to restore brotherly love and respect among our people who have been divided, robbed and spoiled by the American whites.

Judge Duffy has now openly spoken his hatred for any justice coming to us who have turned to do righteousness, which is the fulfillment of the prophecy which reads: "Ye, truth faileth; and judgement is turned away backward and justice standeth afar off [for the so-called Negroes] for truth is fallen in the streets and equity cannot enter. He that departed from evil maketh himself a prey: and the Lord {Master Fard Muhammad] saw it and it displeased Him that there was no judgement [justice]" (Isa. 59:15).

Blessed are the so-called Negroes that depart from the evil and filthy doings of this American white man. How happy they are who seek refuge in Allah and are believers. **Pgs. 321-324 MTBM**

Reference 55 & 56: He Was Sent

John 4:34

"My food," said Jesus, "is to do the will of him who sent me and to finish his work."

Matthew 15:24

"He answered, 'I was sent only to the lost sheep of Israel.'"

The So-Called Negroes Salvation
(Chapter from MTBM By The Honorable Mr. Elijah Muhammad)

The number one principle of belief is that your God is one God and beside Him you have no other god that can help you. I shall begin with this, the most important of all principles of belief.

How many non-Muslims will we find who do not believe in God as being One God? Regardless of the trinity belief practiced by the Christians, they (the Christians) claim and agreed that Allah (God) is One God. They make fools of themselves when they reject Islam and the Muslim's five principals of belief: One God, His prophets, His Books, the Resurrection, The Judgment. How, then, did they (the Christians) go astray believing in three Gods? Nevertheless, they maket one of the three the Father of the other two-and these remaining two the equal of the Father.

The so-called Negroes have been led into the gravest of errors in the knowledge of God (Allah) and the true religion (Islam) by their white slave-masters. They (the so-called Negroes) have been robbed more than any other people on this planet Earth. If they will only read and listen to the simplest of truths of which I write and speak have three essentials in it: power, light and life.

"I am a mortal like you-it is revealed to me that your God is one God (18:110). " Will you not bear witness with Muhammad in the above quoted chapter and verse of the Holy Qur-an?

The white race will not agree with Muhammad and the true religion of God (Allah); which is Islam because of the nature in which they were created, -as they are the opposers of Allah and the Truth. They (white people) know that the so-called Negroes believe in them, but with the help of my God (Allah), -who came in the person of Master W. F. Muhammad we will show up the false with the truth in its plainest simplest form.

It is foolish to believe in three gods-foolish to make Jesus the Son and the equal of His Father (the one of 2,000 years ago). If Jesus said in His suffering "My God, My God, why hast Thou forsaken Me?" (Matthew 27:46) then most surely He did not recognize Himself as being the equal of God, and no other scripture shows Jesus as the equal of God.

If Jesus said that He was sent (Matthew 15:24 and John 4:34), then He cannot claim to be the equal of His sender. God is not sent by anyone; He is a self-sender. He says in Isaiah (44:81-45:22): "Is there a god besides Me? I know not any. "In another place He states, "I am God, there is none else." (Isaiah 46:9). Also, "One God and none other." (Mark 12:32). **Pg. 27 MTBM**

Reference 57: Holy One From Mount Paran

Habakkuk 3:3

"God came from Teman, the Holy One from Mount Paran. His glory covered the heavens and his praise filled the earth."

According to the dictionary of the Bible: Teman, a son of Esau by Adah (Gen. 36:11, 15, 42) and in I Chron. 1:36, now if Habakkuk saw God come or coming from the sons of Esau (Eliphaz), then God must be a man and not a spook. If Habakkuk's (3:3) prophecy refers to some country, town, or city, if there be any truth at all in this prophecy, then we can say that this prophet saw God as a material being, belonging to the human family of the earth-and not to a spirit (ghost).

In the same chapter and verse, Habakkuk saw the Holy One from Mount Paran. This is also earthly, somewhere in Arabia.

Here the Bible makes a difference between God and another person who is called the Holy One. Which one should we take for our God? For one is called God, while another One is called Holy One. The Holy One: His glory covered the heavens and the earth was full of His praise. It has been a long time since the earth was full of praise for a Holy One. Even to this hour, the people do not care for Holy People and will persecute and kill the Holy One, if God does not intervene. **Pg.7 MTBM**

Reference 58: I, the Lord, Thy Saviour

Isaiah 49:24

"Can plunder be taken from warriors, or captives be rescued from the fierce?"

Isaiah 49:25

"But this is what the Lord says:
'Yes, captives will be taken from warriors,
and plunder retrieved from the fierce;
I will contend with those who contend with you,
and your children I will save.'"

Isaiah 49:26

"I will make your oppressors eat their own flesh;
they will be drunk on their own blood, as with wine.
Then all mankind will know
that I, the Lord, am your Savior,
your Redeemer, the Mighty One of Jacob."

Shall you be the winner in the third World War? The God of Justice (The Son of Man, the Great Mahdi) shall be the winner. He is on the side of the so-called Negroes, to free them from you, their killers. As it is written: "Shall the prey be taken from the mighty or the lawful captives delivered? But thus saith the Lord even the captives of the mighty shall be taken away and the prey of the terrible shall be delivered; for I will contend with him that contendeth with thee. I will feed them that oppress thee with their own flesh; and they shall be drunken with their own blood. As with sweet wine and all flesh shall know that I, the Lord, am thy Savior and thy Redeemer." (Isa. 49:24-26).

We, the so-called Negroes, are the prey. Thou are the Mighty, the terrible ones, thanks to Allah, the Greatest, who is with us, to save and deliver us His people -- 20 million members of the Tribe of Shabazz -- who must have some of this earth, that they can call their own. Their God will give it to them. But woe unto you, the unjust judges, for the Son of Man shall destroy thee and give the kingdom to the slave. He is not to come. He is here! Believe it or not, I seek refuge in Him from your evil plannings.
Pg. 299 MTBM

Reference 59: If God Was Your Father

John 8:42

"Jesus said to them, 'If God were your Father, you would love me, for I have come here from God. I have not come on my own; God sent me.'"

IF GOD WAS YOUR FATHER YOU WOULD LOVE ME
(Chapter from MTBM By The Honorable Mr. Elijah Muhammad)

Read and study the above chapter of John 8:42, all of you, who are Christians, believers in the Bible and Jesus, as you say. If you understand it right, you will agree with me that the whole

Caucasian race is a race of devils. They have proved to be devils in the garden of Paradise and were condemned 4,000 years later by Jesus.

Likewise, they are condemned today, by the Great Mahdi Muhammad, as being nothing but devils in the plainest language. The so-called American Negroes have been deceived and blinded by their unlikeness, soft-smooth buttered words, eye-winking, back-patting, a false show of friendship and handshaking.

The above mentioned acts, with the exception of handshaking, by men are a disgrace to any decent intelligent person. Know the truth and be free from such disgrace.

Surely, if the Father of the two peoples, black and white, were the same, the two would love each other because they are of the same flesh and blood.

It is natural then for them to love each other. Again, it is not unnatural then for a member or members of a different race or nation not to love the nonmember of their race or nation as their own.

The nature in which we are created will not allow us to be like that, and it works the same in all things living that have a bit of intelligence, including the birds and beasts.

The argument here between Jesus and the Jews in that the Jews claim they all were the same people disagreed with and proved they were not from the same Father.

He, having knowledge of both Fathers, knew their Father (devil) before his fall and before he had produced his children (the white race), of whom the Jews are members. Here, in this chapter, (John 8), it shows there was no love in the Jews for Jesus. **Pgs. 23-24 MTBM**

Reference 60: In The Beginning

Genesis 1:1

"In the beginning God created the heavens and the earth."

The Bible is now being called the Poison Book by God Himself, and who can deny that it is not poison? It has poisoned the very hearts and minds of the so-called Negroes so much that they can't agree with each other. From the first day that the white race received the Divine Scripture they started tampering with its truth to make it suit themselves, and blind the black man. It is their nature to do evil, and the Book can't be recognized as the pure and Holy Word of God. It opens with the words of someone other than God trying to represent God and His Creation to us. This is called the Book of Moses and reads as follows: In the beginning God created Heaven and Earth (Gen. 1:1). When was this beginning? There in the Genesis the writer tells us that it was 4,004 B.C.. This we know, now, that it refers to the making of the white race, and not the heavens and earth. The second verse of the first chapter of Genesis reads: And the earth was without form and void; darkness was upon the deep and the spirit of God moved upon the face of the waters. What was the water on, since there was no form of earth? Pgs. 94-95 MTBM

Reference 61: Innocent Earth's Blood

Genesis 4:10

"The Lord said, 'What have you done? Listen! Your brother's blood cries out to me from the ground.'"

According to the word of Allah (God) and the history of the world, since the grafting of the Caucasian race 6,000 years ago, they have caused more bloodshed than any people known to the black nation. Born murderers, their very nature is to murder. The Bible and Holy Qur-an Sharrieff are full of teachings of this bloody race of devils. They shed the life blood of all life, even their own, and are scientists at deceiving the black people.

They deceived the very people of Paradise (Bible, Gen. 3:13). They killed their own brother (Gen. 4:8). The innocent earth's blood (Gen. 4:10) revealed it to its Maker (thy brother's blood cryeth unto me from the ground). The very earth, the soil of America, soaked with the innocent blood of the so-called Negroes shed by this race of devils, now crieth out to its Maker for her burden of carrying the innocent blood of the righteous slain upon her. Let us take a look at the devil's creation from the teaching of the Holy Qur-an.

And when your Lord said to the angels, I am going to place in the earth one who shall rule, the angels said: What will Thou place in it such as shall make mischief in it and shed blood, we celebrate Thy praise and extol Thy holiness (Holy Qur-an Sharrieff 2:30).

This devil race has and still is doing just that -- making mischief and shedding blood of the black nation whom they were grafted from. Your Lord said to the angels, "Surely I am going to create a mortal of the essence of black mud fashioned in shape" (Holy Qur-an Sharrieff, 15:28). **Pg. 128 MTBM**

Reference 62: Jehovah Calls Moses

Exodus 3:10

"So now, go. I am sending you to Pharaoh to bring my people the Israelites out of Egypt."

THE BIBLE AND HOLY QUR-AN: WHICH ONE CONTAINS WORDS OF GOD?
(Chapter from MTBM By The Honorable Mr. Elijah Muhammad)

Both books are called holy. The word of Allah (God) is holy, and His word is true. Therefore, all truth is holy; for Allah (God) is holy and is the author of truth, without the shadow of a doubt! Allah is the representative of the Holy Qur-an (not a prophet) in these words: "This book, there is no doubt of it, is a guide to those who guard against evil" (2:2), translated by Maulvi Muhammad Ali. Abdullah Yusuf Ali's translation of the same verse reads nearly the same: "This is the book; in it is guidance, sure, without doubt, to those who fear Allah (God)" (2:2).

The Bible does not claim God to be its author. Jehovah calls to Moses out of the burning bush to go to Pharaoh (Ex. 3:9). There is no mention of a book or Bible that is found that Jehovah gave to Moses in the first five books of the Bible, which are claimed to be Moses' books. Moses' rod is the only thing used against Pharaoh and the land of Egypt; and tables of stone in the mountains of Sinai. The miraculous rod of Moses, and not a book, brought Pharaoh and his people to their doom. The Ten Commandments served as a guide for the Jews in the Promised Land. Where do we find in the Bible that it was given to Moses by Jehovah under such name as Bible or the Book?

But, on the other hand, Allah (God) tells that He gave the Book, the Holy Qur-an, to Muhammad. "I am Allah, the best knower, the revelation of the book there is no doubt in it, it is from the Lord of the worlds." (Sura 32:1,2). Allah says to Muhammad in the same above (Sura 32:23): "We gave the Book to Moses, and be not in doubt in receiving it, we made it a guide for the children of Israel."

(If Moses' rod and book were given as a guide for Israel, and the gospel God gave to Jesus as a guide and warning to the Christians, and the Holy Qur-an to Muhammad for the Arab world, will God give us (the so-called Negroes) a book as a guide for us? Will He bring it or send it? For those books were for other people and not for us.)

If we are in the change of the two worlds (Christianity and Islam), then surely we need a "new book" for our guidance; for those books have served the people to whom they were given. But all or both books are guidance for us all. Yet we must have a new book for the "new change"; that which no eye has seen nor ear has heard, nor has entered into our hearts what it is like. We know these books, they have been seen and handled by both the good and no good. Certainly the Holy Qur-an is from the Lord of the Worlds, there can be no doubt in the word of Allah (God). But if the book or books have the words of someone else other than Allah's words in it or them, there is no doubt in our hearts concerning the receivings of such book or books. **Pgs. 86-87 MTBM**

Reference 63: Knoweth No Man

Matthew 24:36

"But about that day or hour no one knows, not even the angels in heaven, nor the Son, but only the Father."

He is called the "Son of Man," the "Christ," the "Comforter." You are really foolish to be looking to see the return of the Prophet Jesus. It is the same as looking for the return of Abraham, Moses and Muhammad. All of these prophets prophesied the coming of Allah or one with equal power, under many names. You must remember that Jesus could not have been referring to Himself as returning to the people in the last days. He prophesied of another's coming who was much greater than He. Jesus even acknowledged that He did not know when the hour would come in these words; "But of that day and hour knoweth no man, no, not the angels of heaven, but my Father only." (Matt. 24:36).

If He were the one to return at the end of the world, surely He would have had knowledge of the time of His return—the knowledge of the hour. But He left Himself out of that knowledge and placed it where it belonged, as all the others—prophets—had done. No prophet has been able to tell us the hour of the judgment. No one but He, the great all wise God, Allah. He is called the "Son of Man," the "Mahdi", the "Christ". The prophets, Jesus included, could only foretell those things which would serve as signs, signs that would precede such a great one's coming to judge the world. The knowledge of the hour of judgment is with the Executor only.

Pg. 11 MTBM

Reference 64: Lazarus

Read St. Luke Chapter 15

We have made the grave mistake of Lazarus and the Prodigal Son, (St. Luke: Chapter 15), the one who was so charmed over the wealth and food of the rich man that he could not leave his gate to seek the same for himself,- regardless of the disgraceful condition in which the rich man puts him, even to sending his dogs to attack him. The Angels had to come and take him away.

The other (Prodigal Son), being tempted by the loose life of strange women, drinking, gambling, and adultery, caused him to love the stranger's way of life so much so that it cost him all that he originally possessed (self-independence and Divine Guidance).

His Father (God in person) had to come and be his representative to again meet his brothers, family, and friends.

Nothing fits the description of us better, the so called Negroes (Asiatics). Many of us today are so lazy that we are willing to suffer anything rather than go for self. It is true that our God has come to set us in Heaven, but not a Heaven wherein we will not have to work. **Pgs. 25-26 MTBM**

Reference 65: Let Us Make Man

Genesis 1:26

"Then God said, 'Let us make mankind in our image, in our likeness, so that they may rule over the fish in the sea and the birds in the sky, over the livestock and all the wild animals, and over all the creatures that move along the ground.'"

Again, we learn who the Bible (Genesis 1:26) is referring to in the saying: Let us make man. This US was fifty-nine thousand, nine hundred and ninety-nine (59,999) black men and women; making or grafting them into the likeness or image of the original man. **Pg. 118 MTBM**

The Bible is now being called the Poison Book by God Himself, and who can deny that it is not poison? It has poisoned the very hearts and minds of the so-called Negroes so much that they can't agree with each other. From the first day that the white race received the Divine Scripture they started tampering with its truth to make it suit themselves, and blind the black man. It is their nature to do evil, and the Book can't be recognized as the pure and Holy Word of God. It opens with the words of someone other than God trying to represent God and His Creation to us. This is called the Book of Moses and reads as follows: In the beginning God created Heaven and Earth (Gen. 1:1). When was this beginning? There in the Genesis the writer tells us that it was 4,004 B.C.. This we know, now, that it refers to the making of the white race, and not the heavens and earth. The second verse of the first chapter of Genesis reads: And the earth was without form and void; darkness was upon the deep and the spirit of God moved upon the face of the waters. What was the water on, since there was no form of earth? As I see it, the Bible is very questionable. After God had created everything without asking anyone for help then comes His weakness in the 26th verse of the same chapter (Gen. 1:26). He invites us to help Him make a man. Allah has revealed the us that was invited to make a man (white race). A man is far more easy to make than the heavens and earth. We can't charge these questionable readings of the Bible to Musa because he was a prophet of God, and they don't lie. **Pgs. 94-95 MTBM**

Reference 66 & 67: Loosening Of Devil

Revelation 20:7

"When the thousand years are over, Satan will be released from his prison."

Revelation 20:3

"He threw him into the Abyss, and locked and sealed it over him, to keep him from deceiving the nations anymore until the thousand years were ended. After that, he must be set free for a short time."

Revelation 20:8

"And will go out to deceive the nations in the four corners of the earth—Gog and Magog—and to gather them for battle. In number they are like the sand on the seashore."

Revelation 20:9

"They marched across the breadth of the earth and surrounded the camp of God's people, the city he loves. But fire came down from heaven and devoured them."

Revelation 20:10

"And the devil, who deceived them, was thrown into the lake of burning sulfur, where the beast and the false prophet had been thrown. They will be tormented day and night for ever and ever."

Such teaching (a mystery God) that God is a mystery makes the prophets' teachings of God all false. There should be a law made and enforced upon such teachers until they have been removed from the public.

According to Allah, the origin of such teachings as a Mystery God is from the devils! It was taught to them by their father, Yakub, 6,000 years ago. They know today that God is not a mystery but will not teach it. He (devil), the god of evil, was made to rule the nations of earth for 6,000 years, and naturally he would not teach obedience to a God other than himself.

So, a knowledge of the true God of Righteousness was not represented by the devils. The true God was not to be made manifest to the people until the god of evil (devil) has finished or lived out his time, which was allowed to deceive the nations (read These. 2:9-10, Rev. 20:3, 8-10).

The shutting up and loosing of the devil mentioned in Rev. 20:7 could refer to the time between the A.D. 570-1555 when they (John Hawkins) deceived our fathers and brought them into slavery in America, which is nearly 1,000 years that they and Christianity were bottled up in Europe by the spread of Islam and Muhammad (may the peace of Allah be upon him) and his successors.

Their being loose to deceive the nations of the earth would refer to the time (A.D.1555 to 1955) which they were loose (free) to travel over the earth and deceive the people.

Now their freedom is being interfered with, by the Order and Power of the God of Righteousness through the Nation of Righteousness. For the past 6,000 years, the prophets have been predicting the coming of God who would be just and righteous. This righteous God would appear at the end of the world (the world of the white race).

Today, the God of Truth and Righteousness is making Him self manifest, that He is not anymore a mystery (unknown), but is known and can be seen and heard the earth over. **Pgs. 2-3 MTBM**

Reference 67 & 68: Lost Sheep (People) & Prodigal Son

Luke 15:11

"*Jesus continued: 'There was a man who had two sons.'*"

Luke 15:21

"*The son said to him, 'Father, I have sinned against heaven and against you. I am no longer worthy to be called your son.'*"

Luke 15:22

"*But the father said to his servants, 'Quick! Bring the best robe and put it on him. Put a ring on his finger and sandals on his feet.'*"

The so-called American Negroes (my people) are now in a time when they must decide on life or death. The world we have known is on its way out, and it wishes to carry you and me with it.

But, it will not; this is the right path -- believe in Allah and come follow me.

We are the last members of the original Black Nation and have been found and chosen by Allah to make a great nation -- a nation under His guidance to excel the nations of the past.

Study the parable of Jesus and the lost sheep, the prodigal son (Luke 15:11, 21, 22), the stone that the builders rejected, the garden taken from the wicked husband and given to another and the mustard seed becoming a tree under which the beast found shade and in which the birds found rest.

Know that you, the so-called American Negroes, are divinely promised the Kingdom of Heaven (as it is called) after the destruction of this world. The people of this world will stop at nothing in trying to seduce you to follow them and remain with them so that you, too, will share in their doom. They ask you to take part in their doom, and you accept. When accepting the call to their false friendship you are accepting death.

I hope you remember what I said to you concerning the prepared destruction of Allah for this people and you who take part with them. Since they already have a head start, they believe they will deceive you in going along with them, ignoring the call of Allah and your own salvation and heaven at once while you live.

Pg. 297 MTBM

"The journey to understanding is not meant to be traveled alone. Our community welcomes those who seek knowledge and are ready to engage in meaningful discussions about these teachings. Join us and connect with others who are committed to the truth."

 *(https://nwnoicommunity.aitribes.app/ft/axkVr)*

Reference 69: Love One Another

John 15:17

"This is my command: Love each other."

Reference 70: Love The Brotherhood

1 Peter 2:17

"Show proper respect to everyone, love the family of believers, fear God, honor the emperor."

First Love Yourself
(Chapter from MTBM By The Honorable Mr. Elijah Muhammad)

One of the greatest handicaps among the so-called Negroes is that there is no love for self, nor love for his or her own kind. This not having love for self is the root cause of hate (dislike), disunity, disagreement, quarreling, betraying, stool pigeons and fighting and killing one another. How can you be loved, if you have not love for self? And your own nations and dislike being a member of your own, then what nation will trust your love and membership.

You say of yourself, "I love everybody. " This cannot be true. Love for self comes first. The Bible, the book that you claim to believe says, "Love the brotherhood" (I Peter 2:17), "Love one another" (John 15:17). Love of self comes first. The one who loves everybody is the one who does not love anyone. This is the false teaching of the Christians for the Christians war against Christians. They have the Bible so twisted by adding in and taking out of the truth that it takes only God or one whom God has given the knowledge of the Book to understand it.

The Bible puts more stress upon the "love for the thy neighbor" than the "love for the brother." When asked "Who is my neighbor?" The answer was contrary and incorrect. Jesus' answer was that of two men who were on a journey. They were not from the same place. One was from Jerusalem, the other one was a Samaritan. The Samaritan came to where the man from Jerusalem lay wounded by the robbers who had stripped him of his possessions. The Samaritan showed sympathy for the fellow traveler. (He was not a neighbor in the sense of the word. A neighbor can be an enemy.) Many enemies live in the same neighborhood of a good neighbor. But, the answer that Jesus gave was a futile one which could be classified as a parable of the so-called Negroes and their slave-masters.

The so-called Negroes fell into the hands of the slave-masters, who have robbed, spoiled, wounded and killed them. The Good Samaritan here would be the Mahdi (Allah) –God in Person, as He is often referred to by the Christians as the "the second coming of Jesus, or the Son of Man to judge man." This one will befriend the poor (the so-called Negroes) and heal their wounds by pouring into their heads knowledge of self and others and free them of the yoke of slavery and kill the slave- masters, as Jehovah did in the case of Pharaoh and his people to free Israel from bondage and the false religion and gods of Pharaoh.

There were many other proofs in the Bible which agree with the above answer.

Love yourself and your kind. Let us refrain from doing evil to each other, and let us love each other as brothers, as we are the same flesh and blood. In this way, you and I will not have any trouble in uniting. It is a fool who does not love himself and his people. Your black skin is the best, and never try changing its color. Stay away from intermixing with your slave-master's children. Love yourself and your kind. **Pgs. 32-33 MTBM**

Reference 71: Make All Things New

Revelation 21:5

"He who was seated on the throne said, 'I am making everything new!' Then he said, 'Write this down, for these words are trustworthy and true.'"

MAKE ALL THINGS NEW
(Chapter from MTBM By The Honorable Mr. Elijah Muhammad)

"Behold I, (Allah), make all things new and He said unto Me, write: For these words are true and faithful" (Bible, Rev. 21:5)

It is necessary for me to consult or refer to the Bible for this subject. It can be found in the Holy Qur-an, but not in the exact words as are found in the Bible. So, because of the truth of it, and because my people do not know any Scripture or ever read any Scripture other than the Bible (which they do not understand), I thought it best to make them understand the book which they read and believe in, since the Bible is their graveyard and they must be awakened from it. There are many Muslims who do not care to read anything in the Bible. But those Muslims have not been given my job.

Therefore, I ignore what they say and write! By all means, we must get the "truth" to our people (the so-called Negroes), for the time is limited. The coming of a "New World," or a new order of things is very hard for the people of the Old World to believe. Therefore, they are opposed to the New World.

It does not take a wise man to see the necessity of a new order or a new world, since the old one has fulfilled its purpose. Let the Christians' preachers and scientists ponder over the above prophecy of their Bible. If the time comes when Allah (God) will make all things NEW, will the Christians as we see them today be in that which Allah (God) will make NEW? When should we expect Allah (God) to make all things NEW? After the destruction of the wicked, their king and world. Just when should the end of the old world be? The exact day is known only to Allah, but many think that they know the year. But we all know that 1914 was the end of the 6,000 years that was given to the old world of the devils to rule. A religion used by the devils to convert people cannot be accepted by Allah, especially when it did not come from Him.

We all know that Christianity is from the white race. Should we be surprised at this late day to see it come to pass? Think over the saying of your own Bible. "The great deceiver of the nations?" (Rev. 20:3-8). Of course, he deceived them (the so-called Negroes) that had received his mark (the mark of Christianity, the cross).

More than anyone else, those who worship his image (the so-called Negroes) are guilty of loving the white race and all that race stands for. One can even find the pictures of white people on the walls, mantel, shelves, dressers and tables of their homes. Some carry them on their person. The so-called Negroes go to church and bow down to their statues under the name of Jesus and Mary and some under the name of Jesus' disciples, which are only the images of the white race, their arch-deceiver.

They even worship the white race's names, which will not exist among the people of the new world, for they are not the names of God.

The so-called Negroes would greatly benefit themselves if they would seek their places in "that" which Allah (God) makes new by giving back to the great deceiver his religion (Christianity), churches and names and accept the religion of their righteous nation, Islam, a name of their God, which is unlimited in the eyes of any white person.

There is no end to the black nation. That nation will live forever. The so-called Negroes do not know it, and their slave-masters know that they do not know. Therefore, they have the so-called Negroes deceived 100 per cent. It is really pitiful to see how the poor black preachers are blinded and chained by the slave-masters hand and foot. They could not speak or agree with truth even if they wanted to. Come to me, brother preachers, and believe in Allah, the true God and the true religion, Islam! Free yourselves from such chained slavery.

I am very insignificant in your eyes, but I have the keys of God to your problems. You should not fear. The day has come that you will have to seek refuge in (the new world) something better and more enduring than the white race's Christianity. It is not your religion. **Pgs. 82-84 MTBM**

Reference 72: Moses Call Dan A Lion's Whelp

Deuteronomy 33:22

"About Dan he said: 'Dan is a lion's cub, springing out of Bashan.'"

That old serpent, called the devil and Satan, which deceiveth the whole world (Rev. 12:9) is a person or persons whose characteristics are like that of a serpent (snake). Serpents or snakes of the grafted type cannot be trusted, for they will strike you when you are not expecting a strike.

Let us refer to Genesis: Dan shall be a serpent by the way, an adder in the path that bitten the horse's heels so that his rider shall fall backward (Gen. 49:17). Here Jacob on his deathbed fourteenth the future of his sons (Moses calls Dan a lion's whelp; he shall leap from Basin; Duet. 33:22). That old serpent, devil and Satan, the old beast, is the dragon which deceiveth the whole world of the poor ignorant darker nations and has caused them to fall off their mount of prosperity, success and independence by accepting advice, guidance and empty promises which he (the serpent-like Caucasian devil) never intended to fulfill.

How well the prophets have described the characteristics of this race of devils as corresponding to the nature of a snake (serpent). Most snakes wobble and make a crooked trail when and wherever they crawl. So it is with the white race, which goes among the black nation leaving the marks of evil and crooked dealings and doings. **Pgs. 122-123 MTBM**

Reference 73: Nations Set For Showdown

Joel 2:2

"A day of darkness and gloom, a day of clouds and blackness. Like dawn spreading across the mountains a large and mighty army comes, such as never was in ancient times nor ever will be in ages to come."

The years 1965 and 1966 are going to be fateful for America, bringing in the "Fall of America." As one of the prophets of the Bible prophesied in regard to her, "as the morning spreads abroad upon the mountains a great and strong people set in battle array" (Joel 2:2). This is the setting of the nations for a showdown to determine who will live on earth. The survivor is to build a nation of peace to rule the people of the earth forever under the guidance of Almighty God, Allah. With the nations setting forth for a final war at this time, God pleads for His people (the inheritors of the earth, the so-called Negroes).

The so-called Negro is the prey of the white man of America, being held firmly in the white man's power, along with 2 million Indians who must be redeemed at this time and will be, if the so-called Negro turns to His Redeemer. The problem of the American black man is his unwillingness to be separated from his 400-year-old enemies. The problem, therefore, is harder to solve, especially with the enemy trying to fascinate the Negro with his lower class girls and women arraying them partly nude before the Negroes in every public news medium (cheap daily newspapers and magazines, radio and TV) and the Negro is quick to imitate.

Pgs. 270-271 MTBM

Reference 74: Neither Is There Salvation (KKK)

Acts 4:12

"Salvation is found in no one else, for there is no other name under heaven given to mankind by which we must be saved."

Reference 75: No Other God

Isaiah 45:22

"Turn to me and be saved, all you ends of the earth; for I am God, and there is no other."

Mark 12:32

"'Well said, teacher,' the man replied. 'You are right in saying that God is one and there is no other but him.'"

Isaiah 46:9

"Remember the former things, those of long ago; I am God, and there is no other; I am God, and there is none like me."

It is foolish to believe in three gods-foolish to make Jesus the Son and the equal of His Father (the one of 2,000 years ago). If Jesus said in His suffering "My God, My God, why hast Thou forsaken Me?" (Matthew 27:46) then most surely He did not recognize Himself as being the equal of God, and no other scripture shows Jesus as the equal of God.

If Jesus said that He was sent (Matthew 15:24 and John 4:34), then He cannot claim to be the equal of His sender. God is not sent by anyone; He is a self-sender. He says in Isaiah (44:81-45:22): "Is there a god besides Me? I know not any. "In another place He states, "I am God, there is none else." (Isaiah 46:9). Also, "One God and none other." (Mark 12:32). **Pg. 27 MTBM**

Reference 76: Not Know God By His Name

Exodus 6:3

"I appeared to Abraham, to Isaac and to Jacob as God Almighty, but by my name the Lord I did not make myself fully known to them."

What I am trying to make clear is that white people do not believe in Allah and Islam or the prophets of Allah. Why then, should you seek the truth of it from them? You will soon come to know that you should not seek any truth from them. They have you following in the wrong direction and hope to keep you like that; but by my Allah's power and wisdom, and my life's blood, you shall know the Truth even against your own will.

They (white people) have nearly all of the poor black preachers on their side to oppose Allah, myself and Islam, the religion of righteous. They will fail and be brought to disgrace as Pharaoh's magicians and he himself were by Allah (God), for you have not known Him, or His religion, as Israel had not known God by His name Jehovah (Exod. 6:3)

They felt that they should not believe Moses' representation of God by any other name than God Almighty, regardless of Moses' stress upon Jehovah as being the God of their Fathers. Pharaoh had not used that name (Jehovah); so Israel would not accept it until a showdown between Jehovah and Pharaoh. I would not like to have you wait until a showdown between Allah and the modern Pharaoh's people; therefore I come to you with the truth, verifying that which is before it, and giving good news to the believers that they most certainly shall have Heaven in this life. I also come to you with the warning to those who disbelieve that you most certainly shall have hell in this life, and in the hereafter you most certainly will be among the losers, or do they say, "He has forged it?" Nay, it is the truth from the Lord, that you may warn a people to whom no warning has come before, that they may follow the right direction (Holy Qur'an 32-3).

You say, "Who is this Allah, and this religion Islam?" Know my people, the Divine Supreme Being, has 99 attributes that make up His name, and Allah is the 100th. Surely His are the most beautiful names. He will make Himself known to the world that He is God and besides Him there is no God and that I am His Messenger, that Islam is a religion backed by the power of Allah (God) to free you from the hands of your merciless enemies (the slave masters) once and forever.

Allah, your God, will grant you power to overcome your enemies though their power may look as endurable as the mountains. Fear not! Allah is the Best Knower. Armageddon has started, and after it there will be no Christian religion or churches. Jesus was a Muslim, not a Christian. **Pgs. 21-22 MTBM**

Reference 77: 144,000 Return To God

Revelation 14:1

"Then I looked, and there before me was the Lamb, standing on Mount Zion, and with him 144,000 who had his name and his Father's name written on their foreheads."

Today for the first time in our history we have that true friend in Allah (who came in the person of Master Fard Muhammad) and the nation of Islam, if we only would submit and accept Him.

It is written (Rev. 14:1) that 144,000 of us will accept and return to our God and people and the rest of my people will go down with the enemies of Allah. For this sad prophesy of the loss of my people I write what I am writing, hoping perhaps that you may be able to beat the old prophet's predictions by making the truth so simple that a fool can understand it. You must be rightly civilized. You must go back to your own people and country, but not one of you can return with what you have. You must know that this is the time of our separation and the judgement of this world (the Caucasian race) that you and I have known. Therefore, Allah has said to me that the time is ripe for you and me to accept our own (the whole planet earth). What are you waiting for? The destruction? Come, let us reason together, but you cannot until you have a thorough knowledge of self. Who are you waiting for to teach you the knowledge of self? Surely not your slave-masters who blinded you to the knowledge. The white race's civilization will never work for us. **Pg. 46 MTBM**

Reference 78: People Spiritually As Beast

Revelation 12 & 13

These chapters describe the Woman and the Dragon (Revelation 12) and the Beast out of the Sea and the Beast out of the Earth (Revelation 13), detailing cosmic conflict and the rise of the Antichrist. (Read Them)

Accept Your Own
(Chapter from MTBM By The Honorable Mr. Elijah Muhammad)

America has been number one on the list of God for total destruction for a long time; even in the prophesy of Moses, Isaac, Habakkub and Jesus. Her (America) destruction has been coming gradually for the past 34 years.

The nations of the earth are becoming her enemies because of the evils and the murders of the so-called American Negroes, who now could choose to build the kingdom of heaven. There is no let-up in her evil, brutality and murder of her once slaves (the Negro) who are still her slaves mentally. She would not like you to know that the doom is because of the way she treated her slaves. She has deceived everyone who deals with her, as recorded in the Revelations of John of the Bible. Today, she has, as the Revelation of John prophesied, the head of the church (the Pope of Rome) helping her deceive Negroes and keep them in the church so that they may be destroyed with her.

The only thing that will hold the Negro is his belief in whites as a people of divinity. They hold to his religion (Christianity) which they use to deceive everyone they possibly can. It was through Christianity that they got their authority over the black, brown, yellow and red races.

The holding to the white man's name is another chain that carries the Negro down with his enemies. It is laughable and saddening to see the so-called Negro preachers reading and preaching from the Bible while they do not understand it. Negro professionals, scholars and scientists are still ignorant of the fact that as long as they are in the white man's name, they are his slaves. In every nation, as soon as he presents himself in the name of the white man of America or Europe, they know that he is dumb to the fact that he cannot be free until he breaks his slave-master's hold on him - his name, his religion, his way of living and his evil practices. These must be given up before any nation or even God can help or even aid the Negro in becoming a free people recognized by other nations.

Proof has been offered in the name of the present heavyweight champion of the world, Muhammad Ali. It is a divine name - both Muhammad and Ali are the names of God. Quickly, the nations of his kind held out their hands and called to him. Christian black preachers have never been so recognized because of their ignorance in holding the name and religion of their slave-master.

The Revelation of John in the Bible (the Revelator represents them spiritually as beasts because of their savage way of dealing with and murdering black people) and even Isaiah warn you who hold to the white man's names and his religion.

This is your America. We have proven this to you, not your slave-master, that you will get respect and honor throughout the world if you accept your own and take on the names of the divine supreme being. It is in your Bible, and now it has been made manifest to you.

Watch how anxious the white man is to hold you and call you by his name. He still would like to call the champion, Cassius

Clay, after himself, and he would like to call me Poole, after himself. This is to keep the blind, blind; the deaf and the dumb, dumb to the knowledge that even the name alone is sufficient to free you of this evil people.

I have offered America a solution to her problems with her slaves. But because she knows that you are dumb enough not to want to accept it, she is condemning herself to an early doom by rejecting it. The only way out is to separate the two people despite the foolish Negroes' cry that they love white people and want to remain with them.

The time has arrived. The only way to put off for a few more years the total destruction America is to deal fairly with the Negro. But, nevertheless, one day it will come, unless she would like to return to Europe instead of sending the Negro back to Africa.

The whole Western Hemisphere belongs to the darker people, and Europe was given to the white people. Your anger against the Negro getting a just deal has hastened your doom. America will suffer some of the worst calamities within the next year or two - calamities worse than any nation has endured since man has been on earth - that is, if she does not make the right move.

Square up with justice for the slave, and do not try to deceive him through intermarrying your women. Give him up and let him go, or suffer death and destruction. **Pgs. 46-48 MTBM**

Reference 79: Prodigal Son

Luke 15:11-32

This passage is the Parable of the Prodigal Son, where a father's love and forgiveness are emphasized after his son returns home, repentant.

We have made the grave mistake of Lazarus and the Prodigal Son, (St. Luke: Chapter 15), the one who was so charmed over the wealth and food of the rich man that he could not leave his gate to seek the same for himself,- regardless of the disgraceful condition in which the rich man puts him, even to sending his dogs to attack him. The Angels had to come and take him away.

The other (Prodigal Son), being tempted by the loose life of strange women, drinking, gambling, and adultery, caused him to love the stranger's way of life so much so that it cost him all that he originally possessed (self-independence and Divine Guidance). His Father (God in person) had to come and be his representative to again meet his brothers, family, and friends.

Nothing fits the description of us better, the so called Negroes (Asiatics). Many of us today are so lazy that we are willing to suffer anything rather than go for self. It is true that our God has come to set us in Heaven, but not a Heaven wherein we will not have to work. **Pgs. 25-26 MTBM**

Reference 80: Prophecy Of Lost People

Genesis 15:13

"Then the Lord said to him, 'Know for certain that for four hundred years your descendants will be strangers in a country not their own and that they will be enslaved and mistreated there.'"

Reference 81: Prophet Raised From Brethren

Deuteronomy 18:18
"I will raise up for them a prophet like you from among their fellow Israelites, and I will put my words in his mouth. He will tell them everything I command him."

WE NEED NOT HAVE FEAR FOR THE FUTURE
(Chapter from MTBM By The Honorable Mr. Elijah Muhammad)

These above words are those of disbelievers and hypocrites. The disbelievers and hypocrites of prophets and messengers of God never want to give them credit and honor and bear witness with them in saying that the message they are delivering to the people is from the Lord of the Worlds (God).

They always wish to give the lie to what a Divine Messenger or warner brings to the people from God. They say he has forged it or it is of his own making. It is not what God said, it is his saying. These are the words of disbelievers, hypocrites and proud ones against the truth and the bearers of truth.

The above verse says to the Messenger that he is to warn a people to whom no warner has come before him. Many of the writers on the history of Muhammad (may the peace and blessings of Allah be upon him) of nearly 1,400 years ago, write that Muhammad was the first prophet that Mecca had ever seen. Even Maulana Muhammad Ali, who translated the Holy Qur-an in English, says in his References on this verse that Muhammad was the first prophet that Mecca had ever seen and that he was raised among the descendants of Ishmael.

How do the scholars and writers of Islam say such when, if they make Muhammad a descendant of Ishmael they are condemning their own sayings that he was the first prophet of Mecca, when both Abraham and Ishmael were prophets according to the Holy Qur-an. Even the Bible and all religious people recognize Abraham as being a prophet.

Therefore, Muhammad could not have been the prophet, because the very significance of the signs that Abraham and Ishmael built in Mecca tells us much about the type of prophet and people that would be raised up in the last days. So how can they say that this revelation refers to Mecca, the Meccans and Muhammad.

It reads: "Thou mayest warn a people to whom no warner has come before that they may walk aright." This condemns the very fundamental teaching of the origination of the Prophets and Guides for the people coming from that direction, from the East. Mecca has been a sacred place. God, Himself, has protected its sacredness ever since time immemorial.

How then could this be a savage and unknown of the righteous and of even a righteous warner if there were not the will of God to keep that city sacred and deserving as a sign of righteousness?

Then how can the scholars say that it has not even seen a prophet or a warner from Allah? Would Abraham and Ishmael have chosen a more wicked place to set up a sign of the last warner and his people, which the Kaaba and black stone represents?

The very words, "to whom no warner has come before," that they put in a book that is called the last revelation of Allah to the people could not mean Mecca. Because the last warner and the last people to whom prophets and the truth have never come to is the same people that the Bible and Holy Qur-an refer to as being blind, deaf, dumb and (mentally) dead, who must be resurrected before there can be a judgment of the wicked.

No people answers this description better than the American so-called Negroes. And there is no country that better represents that description of where no prophets have been sent than America. As far back as history takes us in reference to America, we find no prophet of Allah preaching Islam or warning the people in the Western Hemisphere of a coming judgment and to submit to the will of Allah that they may be saved from the destruction of that day. It is America.

The prayer of Abraham does not refer to the raising up of a prophet in Arabia, but of a prophet among that particular seed or people of his, who must be searched for, located and found, a teacher must be given to them from Allah to teach and warn them of the purpose of Allah and the purpose of the Messenger being raised among them.

The Bible gives us a very clear prophecy and knowledge of this particular last messenger in many places. It is that he is the first and the last who will be among the people, because they would be the only and last people who would be without the guidance of Allah at the end of the world and must be guided into the path of Allah if they are to be saved from the destruction of the enemies of Allah who had deceived and now hold that people in bondage -- the true descendants of Ishmael of whom Ishmael himself was a prototype and his mother the outcast.

There are many erroneous mistakes made by the scholars and scientists that have caused much misunderstanding of the truth. There are many Arabs throughout the world who cannot bear witness to anyone that another messenger would rise up after Muhammad, who was here nearly 1,400 years ago. This is due to their misunderstanding of the Holy Qur-an and the scriptures of the Prophets Abraham, Moses, Jesus and even Muhammad, himself.

They forget that the Bible prophesies of a lost member of the nation of the original people of the earth, who would be lost somewhere on the earth. But neither the Bible nor the Holy Qur-an specifies the place. The nearest the Bible comes to it is that they would be lost in the wilderness. That fits America.

And Moses says that God told him (Deut. 18:18) "I will raise them up a prophet from among thy brethren like unto thee and will put my words in his mouth and shall speak unto them all that I command him."

This is an answer or a prophecy that compares with the prayer of Abraham -- that God raised up a messenger from among them and taught him the wisdom and the book because his people would not have knowledge of the book and were only guessing at its meaning. This book is referring to the Bible -- that they were guessing at its meaning.

This is true! Thousands of preachers here are preaching the Bible and do not understand the true meaning of it. They only guess at its meaning.

It is not true that the Bible was being taught and preached by the Arab people before Muhammad. The Torah was used among the Jewish people but not in the vicinity of Mecca and its inhabitants. A prophet would be raised among a people and that this man would be like Moses, but the Holy Qur-an and Bible do not give the direct place where this people would be. Moses was raised among his brethren to warn and guide them, and they were the ones who rejected him at first. And it was Moses that God spoke to that a last messenger would be like him.

Moses' people had not had a prophet to come to them from God before the raising up of Moses, and they did not know the scripture because Pharaoh had them worshiping in his false religion. Therefore, Moses had to preach a new God and a new religion to the Hebrews and give them a new concept of God and His religion.

So shall it be with the last messenger. His people must be taught about the true God and that God's true religion which the slave-masters did not teach them. The Holy Qur-an backs up the truth of Allah, that He always raises an apostle from among a people whom He would warn.

If Allah would warn America and the poor slaves who have been blinded and made deaf and dumb by their masters, should not that messenger be one of the so-called Negroes instead of a so-called Negro trying to learn from what Muhammad said to the Arabs nearly 1,400 years ago. This is a guide for us today? It does not stop there.

We have to have something more; therefore, the Holy Qur-an prophesies of another scripture being given, and the Bible also prophesies of another scripture being given in the time of the judgment, because the Holy Qur-an takes us up to the resurrection of the dead but not beyond that.

"Warning a people whom no warner has come before that they may walk aright." It is directed at the American so-called Negroes in North America. As Jesus comes close to revealing the whereabouts of the lost members of a great nation in these words, "that he was sent to the lost sheep of the house of Israel or in the house of Israel." He did not say that he was sent to the lost Israel, but to the lost sheep in the house of Israel. The lost sheep are not Israel. The lost sheep were in the house or government of Israel and were swallowed up by Israel so thoroughly that they were always overlooked.

But we just cannot overlook the prophecy of Ezekiel wherein he prophesies that God said, "Even I will go and search for them, and I will bring them again and settle them in their own land and among their own people."

This is referring to the so-called Negroes. And Isaiah says in his prophecy concerning us that God said He would call them by a new name that He, Himself, would give them, one of His own names, and would take away the names of the enemy and would slay the enemy.

Let us remember that we must understand the truth of prophecy, the sayings of the Holy Qur-an and Bible on this subject, and then place them where they belong and not try to fit them in some place where they do not belong. **Pgs. 248-252 MTBM**

Reference 83: Race Of Devils

Revelation 12:9
"The great dragon was hurled down—that ancient serpent called the devil, or Satan, who leads the whole world astray. He was hurled to the earth, and his angels with him."

Revelation 12:10
"Then I heard a loud voice in heaven say:
'Now have come the salvation and the power and the kingdom of our God,

and the authority of his Messiah.
For the accuser of our brothers and sisters,
who accuses them before our God day and night,
has been hurled down.'"

Revelation 12:11

"They triumphed over him by the blood of the Lamb
and by the word of their testimony;
they did not love their lives so much
as to shrink from death."

Revelation 12:12

"Therefore rejoice, you heavens
and you who dwell in them!
But woe to the earth and the sea,
because the devil has gone down to you!
He is filled with fury,
because he knows that his time is short."

Revelation 12:13

"When the dragon saw that he had been hurled to the earth, he pursued the woman who had given birth to the male child."

Revelation 12:14

"The woman was given the two wings of a great eagle, so that she might fly to the place prepared for her in the wilderness, where she would be taken care of for a time, times and half a time, out of the serpent's reach."

Revelation 12:15

"Then from his mouth the serpent spewed water like a river, to overtake the woman and sweep her away with the torrent."

Revelation 12:16

"But the earth helped the woman by opening its mouth and swallowing the river that the dragon had spewed out of his mouth."

Revelation 12:17

"Then the dragon was enraged at the woman and went off to wage war against the rest of her offspring—those who keep God's commands and hold fast their testimony about Jesus."

Reference 83 & 84: Race Of Devils

2 Thessalonians 2:3

"Don't let anyone deceive you in any way, for that day will not come until the rebellion occurs and the man of lawlessness is revealed, the man doomed to destruction."

2 Thessalonians 2:4

"He will oppose and will exalt himself over everything that is called God or is worshiped, so that he sets himself up in God's temple, proclaiming himself to be God."

2 Thessalonians 2:5

"Don't you remember that when I was with you I used to tell you these things?"

2 Thessalonians 2:6

"And now you know what is holding him back, so that he may be revealed at the proper time."

2 Thessalonians 2:7

"For the secret power of lawlessness is already at work; but the one who now holds it back will continue to do so till he is taken out of the way."

2 Thessalonians 2:8

"And then the lawless one will be revealed, whom the Lord Jesus will overthrow with the breath of his mouth and destroy by the splendor of his coming."

2 Thessalonians 2:9

"The coming of the lawless one will be in accordance with how Satan works. He will use all sorts of displays of power through signs and wonders that serve the lie,"

2 Thessalonians 2:10

"and all the ways that wickedness deceives those who are perishing. They perish because they refused to love the truth and so be saved."

2 Thessalonians 2:11

"For this reason, God sends them a powerful delusion so that they will believe the lie"

2 Thessalonians 2:12

"and so that all will be condemned who have not believed the truth but have delighted in wickedness."

    Remember the Bible's teaching of this race of devils, and especially II Thessalonians (Chapter 2:3-12), and Revelation (12:9-17,20:10). The treatment of the so-called Negroes by the devils is sufficient proof to the so-called Negroes, that they (the white race), are real devils.

And if this teaching, along with what they are suffering from their beloved devils, does not awaken them to the knowledge of the devils, all I can say for them, then is that they are just lost. They won't be accepted by God nor by the righteous Muslims, with even the name of the devils. **Pg. 106 MTBM**

Reference 87: Redemption Of So-Called Negro

Deuteronomy 18:15

"The Lord your God will raise up for you a prophet like me from among you, from your fellow Israelites. You must listen to him."

Deuteronomy 18:18

"I will raise up for them a prophet like you from among their fellow Israelites, and I will put my words in his mouth. He will tell them everything I command him."

Matthew 25:32

"All the nations will be gathered before him, and he will separate the people one from another as a shepherd separates the sheep from the goats."

Revelation 14

This chapter describes the 144,000 standing with the Lamb on Mount Zion, the three angels and their messages, the judgment of the earth, and the harvesting of the earth by the Son of Man. (Read This Chapter)

The so-called Negro is the prey of the white man of America, being held firmly in the white man's power, along with 2 million Indians who must be redeemed at this time and will be, if the so-called Negro turns to His Redeemer. The problem of the American black man is his unwillingness to be separated from his

400-year-old enemies. The problem, therefore, is harder to solve, especially with the enemy trying to fascinate the Negro with his lower class girls and women arraying them partly nude before the Negroes in every public news medium (cheap daily newspapers and magazines, radio and TV) and the Negro is quick to imitate.

The problem between these two people, separating and dignifying the so-called Negroes so they may be accepted and respected as equals or superiors to other nations, must be solved. This is God's promise to the so-called Negro (the lost and found members of the original Black Nation of the earth). This promise was made through the mouths of His prophets (Bible and Qur-an), that He would separate us from our enemies, dignify us and make us the masters after this wicked race has been judged and destroyed for its own evils.

But, as I said, the solving of this problem, which means the redemption of the Negro, is hard to do, since he loves his enemies (See Bible; Deut. 18:15, 18; Psalms; Isaiah; Matthew 25:32; and Revelations, Chapter 14).

The manifestation of Allah and judgment between the so-called Negro and the enemy of God and Nation of Islam will make the so-called Negro see and know his enemy and himself, his people, his God and his religion.

We hear the statement of black educational, political and Christian classes, which express their love for the white man, publicly asking to be his brothers, if not his brothers-in-law. Now, this class wants to make it clear to the world that they really love the white race and not the black race. This means they want to be white instead of black. The devils have made them hate black. They reject the thought of black ever being the ruler or equal with the ruler. They ask boldly for inferiority, not only for themselves, but for their people.

They want to absorb themselves and their kind (especially the so-called American Negro) into the race of white people, thus ending the black race. It is just the opposite with Allah (God), myself and my followers. We "want out completely." We want no claim to kinship with a people who, by nature, are not our kin. Read from Genesis to the Revelation in the Bible and from Sura 2 to Sura 114 of the Holy Qur-an. **Pgs. 271-272 MTBM**

Reference 88: Religion Of Peace

2 Thessalonians 3:16

"Now may the Lord of peace himself give you peace at all times and in every way. The Lord be with all of you."

Psalms 85:8

"I will listen to what God the Lord says; he promises peace to his people, his faithful servants—but let them not turn to folly."

Psalms 29:11

"The Lord gives strength to his people; the Lord blesses his people with peace."

Islam has five beautiful fundamental principles of belief. The most essential of them all is "The belief in One God." This was the belief (Oneness of God) and preachings of the prophets of God from Noah to Muhammad (the last). As I have said, if your religion's roots are not found in the universal order of things, it is not from Allah (God). I defy any opposer to prove the religion (as we know it today) called Christianity to be the religion of God and his prophets Noah, Abraham, Lot, Moses, David and Jesus.

What is Islam? It can be answered in one world -- righteousness. Briefly, it is the religion of Allah (God) and His

Prophets. Islam is as old as Allah (God) Himself and is the religion of which Allah (God) is the author. Islam is the religion of Adam, Noah, Moses, Jesus, and Muhammad (the last). Islam is the religion of entire submission to the will of Allah (God). Islam is the religion which the Holy Qur-an teaches.

Allah (God) says, "This day I have perfected for you your religion, completed my favor on you and chosen for you Islam as a religion" (Chapter 5:3). Allah (God) also says in another chapter of the Holy Qur-an, "Surely the true religion with Allah is Islam" (Chapter 3:18).

The significance of the name "Islam" is peace, the true religion. It is a religion of eternal peace. We cannot imagine Allah (God) offering to us a religion other than one of peace. A religion of peace coming to the righteous after the destruction of the wicked is also mentioned in several places in the Bible: "The Lord will bless His people with peace." (Psa. 29:11): also, "He will speak peace unto His people and to His saints" (Psa. 85:8) and "the Lord of Peace give you peace always" (II Thess. 3:16).

Islam is the religion referred to in the above-mentioned Biblical verses. It is the only religion that gives the believer a peace of mind and contentment. It removes grief and fear at once on believing: "Yea, whoever submits himself entirely to Allah and he is the doer of good to others, he has his reward from his Lord and there is no fear for him, nor shall he grieve" (Holy Qur-an 2:112).

Allah invites to the abode of peace (Holy Qur-an 10:25). Can you imagine a divine prophet being sent with anything other than a religion of peace to his people?

Our people, the so-called American Negroes, will love Islam when they learn more of it. For it is the religion of their fathers, and it is the last of the three great religions on earth. The other two Buddhism and Christianity, cannot give us a lasting peace. We have tried them to our disappointment.

Christianity is one of the most perfect black-slave-making religions on our planet. It has completely killed the so-called Negroes mentally.

Now it takes Allah (God) Himself to revive and restore our people back into their own. Though I am His Messenger, and Allah can use my life as He pleases for them, they are my people and many -- while I am only one.

Islam will give them the heaven while they live. Islam has more to offer than the white-controlled Christianity. Islam is universal. The true believers of Islam are equal in number to the total population of the whites on our planet (400 million).

By nature, all members of the black nation are Muslims (lovers of peace), who number is over the billion mark.

We must have Islam as our religion to restore our peace after suffering under the slavery, the persecutors, and the grievous of wars for 6,000 years. The so-called Negroes of America, who have never known the way of peace, who have never had love or mercy shown to them, today have Allah (God).

The God of mercy is on their side in the religion of Islam. But they are so dumb about it that it hurts my very heart. I am not surprised at what disbeliever's think and say of me, but when a supposed brother Muslim joins the disbeliever's against what I write, then I am surprised. For no true Muslim will speak against another Muslim to the delight of the disbelieving people of Allah and His prophets and the religion of Islam. **Pgs. 69-70 MTBM**

Reference 89: Rest From Fear

Isaiah 14:3

"On the day the Lord gives you relief from your suffering and turmoil and from the harsh labor forced on you..."

The Lord of the world's Finder of we the loss members of the Asiatics Black Nation for 400 years said that the slave-masters put fear in our Fathers when they were babies. Allah is the only one that can remove this fear from us, but he will not remove it from us until we submit to His will, not our will, and fear Him and Him alone. Then, as it is written, "And it shall come to pass in the day that the Lord shall give thee rest from sorrow and from thy fear, and from the hard bondage wherein thou wast made to serve."(Isaiah 14:3). There are so many places that I could point out in the Bible and Holy Qur-an that warn us of fearing our enemies above or equal to the fear of Allah (God). It is a fool who has greater fear of the devils (white man) than Allah who has the power to destroy the devils and their followers (Revelation 21:8; Holy Qur-an 7:18 and 15:43).

We must remember that if Islam means entire submission to the will of Allah, that and that alone is the True religion of Allah. Do not you and your religious teachers and the Prophets of old teach that the only way to receive God's help or Guidance is to submit to his will! -then WHY NOT ISLAM! It (Islam) is the true religion of Allah and the ONLY way to success. Pgs. 29-30 MTBM

Reference 90: Sacrifice Sons And Daughters Unto Devils

Psalms 106:37

"They sacrificed their sons and their daughters to false gods."

Reference 98: Should Not Worship Up Devils

Revelation 9:20

"The rest of mankind who were not killed by these plagues still did not repent of the work of their hands; they did not stop worshiping demons, and idols of gold, silver, bronze, stone and wood—idols that cannot see or hear or walk."

Do thank Allah for revealing this evil deceitful open enemy, "the devil!" The devil has deceived most of the world of black people. They have nearly nine-tenths of the black people headed to their doom with them. Curse be to the black man or woman who loves this open enemy, the devil, and hates his own black skin and kind! May the chastisement of Allah choke you until you submit that: Thee is no God but Allah and that Muhammad in the wilderness of North America is His Messenger! After all of this evil we have suffered at the very hands of these devils, we have become a Nation in a Nation. We must now be separated from them and given a place on this earth that we can call our own!

They, the white race, cannot treat you and me with justice and equality. They cannot do so among themselves. Even though they are against us. This does not mean that they have love and peace for each other. No! They war against each other all the time. They are devils. No heart of love and mercy are in them as you may think. Nature did not give them such a heart.

The Bible warns us against the love and worship of these devils. Psalms 106:37, says "Yea, they sacrificed their sons and their daughters unto devils." In another place it states, "And I would not that you should have fellowship with devils. Ye cannot drink the cup of the Lord, and the cup of the devils: ye cannot be partakers of the Lord's table and of the table of the devils. (1 Cor. 10:-21). "They should not worship up devils" (Rev. 9:20).

The so-called Negroes, because of their fear and ignorance of this real open enemy devil, will fall victim to them if we do not constantly warn them of the consequences.

I am willing to die for the so-called Negro that they may see and understand the truth of self, God and this race of devils.

We have served them well through ignorance and blindness because of being without a teacher. Allah (God) has given you one. I, Elijah Muhammad am from God, Himself! Why not believe and follow me? Are you afraid of being persecuted for the sake of truth to this 22 million blind, deaf and dumb lost-found Nation of Islam? In that case, your life is already doomed. **Pgs. 231-232 MTBM**

Reference 91: Same In Last Judgment

Matthew 24:37

"As it was in the days of Noah, so it will be at the coming of the Son of Man."

Matthew 24:38

"For in the days before the flood, people were eating and drinking, marrying and giving in marriage, up to the day Noah entered the ark;"

Matthew 24:39

"and they knew nothing about what would happen until the flood came and took them all away. That is how it will be at the coming of the Son of Man."

The prophets teach us to let the past judgments of people, their cities, and their warner's serve as a lesson, or sign of the last judgment and its warner's. Noah did not know the hour of the flood. Lot did not know the Hour of Sodom and Gomorrah until the Executors had arrived, and Jesus prophesied; (Matt.24:37-39), "it will be the same in the last judgment of the world of Satan." You have gone astray because of your misunderstanding of the scripture, the Prophet Jesus, and the coming of God to judge the world. My corrections are not accepted.

Your misunderstanding and misinterpretation of it is really the joy of devils. For it is the devils' desire to keep the so-called Negroes ignorant of the truth of God until they see it with their eyes. The truth of God is the salvation and freedom of the so called Negroes from the devils' power.

Can you blame them? No! Blame yourself for being so foolish as to allow the devils to fool you in not accepting the truth after it comes to you. The devils have tried to deceive the people all over the earth with Christianity, that is, God the Father, Jesus the Son, the Holy Ghost; three Gods into One God. The resurrection of the Son and His return to judge the world; or that the Son is in some place above the earth, sitting on the right-hand side of the Father, waiting until the Father makes His enemies His footstool. The period of waiting is 2,000 years. Yet, He died for the Father to save His enemies (the whole world of sinners).

My friends, use a bit of common sense. First, could a wonderful flesh and blood body, made of the essence of our earth, last 2,000 years on the earth, or off the earth, without being healed! Second, where exists such a heaven, of the earth, that flesh and blood of the earth can exist, since the Bible teaches that flesh and blood cannot enter heaven? (Cor. 15:50)

Flesh and blood cannot survive without that of which it is made, the earth. Jesus' prophesy of the coming of the Son of Man is very clear, if you rightly understand. First, this removes all doubt about who we should expect to execute judgment, for if man is to be judged and rewarded according to his actions, who could be justified in sitting as judge of man's doings but another man? How could a spirit be our judge when we cannot see a spirit? And ever since life was created, life has had spirit. But the Bible teaches that God will be seen on the Day of Judgment. Not only the righteous will see Him, but even His enemies shall see Him. **Pgs. 11-12 MTBM**

"How have these insights impacted you so far? Share your reflections and connect with like-minded believers in our private growing community. Your voice and perspective matter."

📌 *https://nwnoicommunity.aitribes.app/ft/axkVr*

Reference 92: Saw God As Material Being

Habakkuk 3:3

"God came from Teman, the Holy One from Mount Paran. His glory covered the heavens and his praise filled the earth."

Reference 93: Saw God Coming

1 Chronicles 1:36

"The sons of Esau: Eliphaz, Reuel, Jeush, Jalam, and Korah."

According to the dictionary of the Bible: Teman, a son of Esau by Adah (Gen. 36:11, 15, 42) and in I Chron. 1:36, now if Habakkuk saw God come or coming from the sons of Esau (Eliphaz), then God must be a man and not a spook. If Habakkuk's (3:3) prophecy refers to some country, town, or city, if there be any truth at all in this prophecy, then we can say that this prophet saw God as a material being, belonging to the human family of the earth-and not to a spirit (ghost).

In the same chapter and verse, Habakkuk saw the Holy One from Mount Paran. This is also earthly, somewhere in Arabia. Here the Bible makes a difference between God and another person who is called the Holy One. Which one should we take for our God? For one is called God, while another One is called Holy One. The Holy One: His glory covered the heavens and the earth was full of His praise. It has been a long time since the earth was full of praise for a Holy One. Even to this hour, the people do not care for Holy People and will persecute and kill the Holy One, if God does not intervene.

In the fourth verse of the above chapter, it says, "He had horns coming out of his hands: and there was the hiding of His power." Such science to represent the God's power could confuse the ignorant masses of the world. Two gods are here represented at the same time. (It is good that God makes Himself manifest to the ignorant world today.) **Pgs. 7-8 MTBM**

Reference 94: Seek Kingdom Of Heaven

Luke 12:31

"But seek his kingdom, and these things will be given to you as well."

Reference 97: Shall Not Live By Bread Alone

Matthew 4:4

"Jesus answered, 'It is written: Man shall not live on bread alone, but on every word that comes from the mouth of God.'"

The Lord's Prayer, as it is called, contains some words that should not have been written there, such as: "Lead us not into temptation." God will not lead us into temptation. It is the devils that tempt us to sin. The above words show a lack of confidence in God to lead us aright, that He must be reminded just how to lead us.

Another is: "Give us this day our daily bread." Here again, the words "this day" could lead one to believe that on that day the prayer was given, there was a shortage of bread, or that the Christians' prayers seek their physical bread first and spiritual bread last, even though the Bible says "You first seek the Kingdom of Heaven and all these things shall be added unto you" (Luke 12:31). In another place it says "Man shall not live by bread alone, but by every word that proceedeth out of the mouth of God" (Matthew 4:4).

These scriptures are contrary to the prayer, although it stands true of the Christians who seek bread, swine's flesh (the poison), whiskey, wine and beer first, and pray for spiritual food last.

The Bible shows (Exodus 16:2,3,8) that it was the want of bread and meat first of all that gave Moses and Aaron much trouble trying to lead the people into the spiritual knowledge of Jehovah and self-independence. They even said when they were hungry: "Would to God we had died by the hand of the Lord in the land of Egypt" (Exodus 16:3).

Ofttimes, they angered Moses and Aaron by their longing for the food of their slave-masters even while on their way to freedom and self-independence.

The Muslims pray in their oft-repeated prayer to seek Allah's help in guiding them on the right path, the path of those whom God has favored and not on the path of those who have caused His anger to descend upon them (the Jews and Christians). This want of the slave-masters bread, meat and luxuries is depriving the so called Negroes today of their independence.

"O Allah, we beseech Thy help and ask Thy protection. We believe in Thee and trust in Thee. We worship Thee in the best manner and we thank Thee. We are not ungrateful to Thee and we cast off and forsake him who disobeys Thee. O Allah, Thee do we serve and to Thee do we pray and make obeisance. To Thee do we flee and we are quick. We hope for Thy mercy and we fear Thy chastisement, for surely Thy chastisement overtakes the unbelievers."

We now see the lost-found members of the great Black Nation, the original people of the sun, are greatly improving their prayer services and obedience to Almighty God Who, in the Person of Master Fard Muhammad, founded them and to Whom praises are due forever for bringing us Islam, the knowledge of God, our Friend, and the devil, our enemy.

To my people in America who bow in submission to Allah's will, He declares He will set us in heaven at once on our acceptance of Him as our God: money, good homes, and friendship in all walks of life. Read for yourself the promised reward and blessings prophesied in the Bible and Holy Qur-an for us who turn to Allah in the last days of the world of the infidels. **Pgs. 154-155 MTBM**

Reference 95: Serpent As A Deceiver

Revelation 12:9

"The great dragon was hurled down—that ancient serpent called the devil, or Satan, who leads the whole world astray. He was hurled to the earth, and his angels with him."

The Bible's forbidden tree (Gen. 2:17) was a tree of the knowledge of good and evil. This also tells us that the tree was person, for trees know nothing! This tree of knowledge was forbidden to Adam and Eve. The only one whom this tree could be is the devil. After deceiving Adam and his wife, he has been called a serpent due to his keen knowledge of tricks and his acts of shrewdness; he made his acquaintance with Adam and his wife in the absence of God. Since this is the nature of a liar, he can best lie to the people when truth is absent.

We know that there was never a time when an actual serpent (or snake) could talk and deceive people in the knowledge of God's law. This same serpent is mentioned in Revelation 12:9 as a deceiver. There (12:9) it is made clear to us that the serpent is The dragon, devil and satan which deceiveth the whole world. In Gen. (3:1) he appeared in the Garden of Paradise before the woman and deceived her (Rev. 12:4). He stood before the woman who was ready to be delivered to devour her child as soon as it is born.

The serpent, the devil, dragon, satan, seems to have been seeking the weaker part of man (the woman) to bring to naught the man -- the Divine Man. It is his first and last trick to deceive the people of God through the woman or with the woman. He is using his woman to tempt the black man by parading her half-nude before his eyes and with public love-making, indecent kissing and dancing over radio and television screens and throughout their public papers and magazines. He is flooding the world with propaganda against God and His true religion, Islam. He stands before the so-called Negro woman to deceive her by feigning love and love-making with her, give the so-called Negro woman preference over her husband or brother in hiring.

In some cities, the Negro woman receives as much higher salary than the so-called Negro man. The devil takes the so-called Negro woman and puts his hands and arms around her body. She may be married or single, it makes no difference. Whenever he can he is making eyes at her. This is an outright destruction of the moral principles of the black man.

In some cities, we convert five to one woman. The so-called Negroes should unite and put a stop to the destruction of their women by the serpent. The woman in (Rev. 12:4) actually refers to the last Apostle of God, and her child refers to his followers, or the entire Negro race as they are called, who are not ready to be delivered (go to their own). Pgs. 126-127 MTBM

Reference 99: Showdown Between Forces Of World And Allah

Joel 3:2

"I will gather all nations and bring them down to the Valley of Jehoshaphat. There I will put them on trial for what they did to my

inheritance, my people Israel, because they scattered my people among the nations and divided up my land."

Joel 3:3

"They cast lots for my people and traded boys for prostitutes; they sold girls for wine to drink."

Reference 101: So-called Negro And His Enemy

Joel 3:7

"See, I am going to rouse them out of the places to which you sold them, and I will return on your own heads what you have done."

It is clear that the armies of the nations of the earth have geared themselves for a showdown between their forces and Allah and the Nation of Islam. We, the so-called American Negroes, the lost and found members of our Nation, are in this decision. The second and third verses of this same chapter (Chapter 3) read like this: "I will also gather all nations and will bring them down into the valley of Jehoshaphat [Europe and Asia -- between black and white] and will please with them there for my people and for my heritage [the lost and found, so-called Negroes], Israel whom they have scattered among the nations and parted by land [between the European white race] and they have casted lots for my people and have given a boy for a harlot and sold a girl for wine that they might drink" (Joel 3:2, 3).

American has fulfilled this to the very letter and spirit with her slaves (the so-called Negroes) under the type of Israel. The Egyptians did nothing of the kind of Israel when they were in bondage to them. In fact, and as God taught me, the Bible is not referring to those people as His People, it is referring to the so-called Negro and his enemy (the white race). The seventh verse also gives us a hint in this way:

"Behold, I will raise them out of the place where you have sold them and will return our recompence upon your own head." (Joel 3:7).

The slave-masters of our fathers must reap what they have sown Allah calls them to war in the ninth verse of the same chapter.

"Proclaim you among the Gentiles, prepare war, wake up the mighty men, let all of the men of war draw near, let them come up." (Joel 3:9).

All the mighty men of science and modern warfare have been called in an effort to devise instruments and weapons against God and the armies of heaven. The nations of the earth are angry. The disbelievers and hypocrites of my people also are angry over the change of the old world to a new world of justice and righteousness, causing much spiritual darkness and misunderstanding to fall upon them. They want to judge the person Allah should choose for His Messenger. **Pg. 268 MTBM**

Reference 100: Signs Of God's Coming

Matthew 24:2

"'Do you see all these things?' he asked. 'Truly I tell you, not one stone here will be left on another; every one will be thrown down.'"

Matthew 24:4

"Jesus answered: 'Watch out that no one deceives you.'"

Matthew 24:5

"For many will come in my name, claiming, 'I am the Messiah,' and will deceive many."

Matthew 24:6

"*You will hear of wars and rumors of wars, but see to it that you are not alarmed. Such things must happen, but the end is still to come.*"

THE FULFILLMENT OF PROPHECIES SEEN
(Chapter from MTBM By The Honorable Mr. Elijah Muhammad)

The Signs of the Coming of God -- "And Jesus said unto them see ye not these things? Verily I say unto you, There shall not be left here one stone upon another, that shall not be torn down"
[Matt.24:2,4-6]

This chapter refers to the signs of the judgment of the wicked world. Jesus pointed out examples of the destruction of the Jewish Temple or synagogue, and the historians wrote that the Romans came about 70 years later -- after the death of Jesus -- and sacked Jerusalem. Really, this was not the end of Jesus' prophecy of the destruction of Jerusalem by the Romans for all the stones were not overthrown by Rome.

This had reference to the end of the whole world of the wicked. Let us take note of his words in the fourth and fifth verses: "Take heed that no man deceive you for many shall come in my name saying I am Christ and shall deceive many."

This did not happen before the destruction of Jerusalem by the Romans. This refers to the entire period of 2,000 years after his (Jesus) death. It is referring to the many who would come and try to imitate him and shall deceive many, especially the very ignorant people who are given to superstition, who can be easily deceived, and they will sometimes add to a leaders title whom they are not serving.

For instance, the ancient Romans were so ignorant and superstitious of the Divine Supreme Being that they made God for themselves out of stones, wood, bulls and the stars of heaven, such as Venus. They still have in the Vatican, so I am told, an image of a calf made of pure gold.

It is the Pope of Rome today whom the church accepts as its intercessor between and Christians and God. And all Catholics, such as priests and cardinals profess to have the power to pray the soul out of purgatory.

All of this is completely out of line with the true worship of God. The Pope takes his place as the head of the Christian church, while the church at the same time claims Jesus Christ to be its head. But in reality, they recognize the Pope (Father) as being their head.

Of course, this is more true, because Jesus was not the head of any church. The church was organized by the Romans. According to history, and not by Jesus. And the truth of this is that it (the church) does not have any Divine power for anyone. If the Christians were not backed by the white man's money, guns, power and bombs, the church would have no power at all. Here many are deceived by the millions in bowing to the head of the church -- the Pope of Rome.

The late Pope who recently died, according to history used to be a soldier and then a general. He fought in wars and did many other acts of unrighteousness before taking his place as the head of the church.

"Many shall come in my name." This does not mean every little local fellow. It means people who get national and world fame by claiming themselves to be Jesus Christ or God.

There have been many who have risen up in Islam in the past who went in the name of the Mahdi but were not the true Mahdi. Even to the late Maulan Muhammad Ali, who also claimed himself to have been Christ, the Messiah, when he was among the Christians, the Jews, Hindu, and among the Muslims, their Mahdi.

Today, that has all been hushed up and passed. The world does not look to him as having been their Mahdi or the Christian's Messiah. Old Orthodox Christians, like old orthodox Hebrews have expected a return to their once great spiritual leaders or prophets, Moses and Jesus, who taught, as the Christians teach today, a return of the Jesus at the end of the world.

Old Orthodox Muslims preach a return of Muhammad of 1,400 years ago, or that there will be no need of another prophet after him, for he settled everything. They do not take the slightest thought that these prophets could not have been the last who would usher in the Judgment. There have been so many things that have come to pass since that time that someone is needed to enlighten the people as to these latest events and to serve as a guide for the people into the presence of God.

What the Prophets brought to the people 4,000 years ago was for that people for the next 2,000 years to the birth of Jesus. And what Jesus brought (the Injil or New Testament) was to last until the end of the world – that is, the time and destruction of the wicked world ruled by satan and the setting up a new universal government under the guidance of Allah or Mahdi, sometimes called the Great Mahdi, to make a distinction from the many others who would be called by such name, as there are many Muslims who have adopted "Mahdi," like the many Italians who have adopted "Jesus" for their names.

The next verse (six) tells us that Jesus had in mind the end of the entire world and not Jerusalem. It reads like this: "And ye shall hear of wars and rumors of wars, see that ye be not troubled, for all these things must come to pass, but the end is not yet."

The wars mentioned in the sixth verse, the nations rising against nations, kingdoms against kingdoms, the famines and pestilence and earthquakes mentioned in the seventh verse, are what we must expect to take place before the end. **Pgs. 286-288 MTBM**

"The journey to understanding is not meant to be traveled alone. Our community welcomes those who seek knowledge and are ready to engage in meaningful discussions about these teachings. Join us and connect with others who are committed to the truth."

📌 *https://nwnoicommunity.aitribes.app/ft/axkVr*

Reference 102: Son Of Man

2 Thessalonians 2:8

"And then the lawless one will be revealed, whom the Lord Jesus will overthrow with the breath of his mouth and destroy by the splendor of his coming."

2 Thessalonians 2:9

"The coming of the lawless one will be in accordance with how Satan works. He will use all sorts of displays of power through signs and wonders that serve the lie."

THE COMING OF ALLAH (GOD)
(Chapter from MTBM By The Honorable Mr. Elijah Muhammad)

The reality of God. I have been and still am trying to make clear to you how important it is. This knowledge of the True God, the reality of God has been and is even now a mystery to the world of mankind with a few exceptions. The day has come that all mankind MUST know the reality of Allah (God)

"There can be no judgment of the people until this knowledge has been given to the people." How can we serve a God without knowledge of Him? My people, the so-called Negroes (The Tribe of Shabazz), are the worst off when if comes to the reality of God.

The whole world has been and is looking for the coming of God. Several places in both the Bible and the Holy Qur-an refer to the coming of Allah (God). "The Coming of the Son of Man." Referring to God as the Son of Man should remove all doubts as to his being anything other than a man.

The Bible mentions Him as the Son of Man and also mentions Him as not being a man but a spirit. On one side He is made clear and on the other He is made a mystery. Representation such as this causes confusion in understanding. We are blind to the knowledge of God when we make Him a mystery and unreal.

Anyone so blind to the reality of God is the servant of the devil, until he or she sees God as a reality. Thousands of years the devil has been blinding man to God's reality, and that is the reason why God had to come in person (and He has), to clear us of such ignorance and blindness to the knowledge of Him.

Therefore, we have the "Coming of Allah (God)." He is referred to as the Son of Man because, first, He is the Son of Man and gotten for a special purpose, which is to return the lost back to their own and to punish and destroy the wicked for their destruction of the righteous, that the righteous may live in peace and do the will of the God of righteousness, free from trouble and interference. Second, He must be a man to deal with man, and we cannot receive or respect other than man.

Since His work is to destroy the wicked. He must remain hidden from the eyes of the world until the time is ripe (the end), for the two (God and devil) cannot rule together.

8 The Son of man (Allah) must wait until His time, after the works of the devil. (II Thessalonians 2:8-9; Holy Our-an 7:14-18). And another place in the Holy Qur'an describes them as the people with the blue eyes. Holy Qur'an 20:102).

Third, the reality of God is as clear as the reality of the devil, but we did not know it until His coming to judge the world. For instance, if we take God for something other than a man (not the man devil), we cannot prove it. If we believe that He Is a spirit and not a man, then we can never expect to have any knowledge of Him except by the sense of feel.

We cannot see a spirit; therefore, the teachings of His coming would be false. The spirit of life is and has been with us all of our lives. God is in person among us today. He is a man, He is in His time. God sees, hears, knows, wills, acts and is a person (man). The evil workings of the devil MUST come to an end. **Pgs. 13-15 MTBM**

Reference 103: Son Of Man Coming

<mark>*Matthew 24:30*</mark>

"Then will appear the sign of the Son of Man in heaven. And then all the peoples of the earth will mourn when they see the Son of Man coming on the clouds of heaven, with power and great glory."

The Coming of the Son of Man
(Chapter from MTBM By The Honorable
Mr. Elijah Muhammad)

"And then shall appear the sign of the Son of Man in heaven; and then shall all of the tribes of the earth mourn, and they shall see the son of Man coming in the clouds of heaven with power and great glory." [Matt.24:30]

Here in the plainest words is the Son of Man on the Judgment Day. We are not told by either Moses or Jesus to look for God on Judgment Day to be anything other than man. Spirits and spooks cannot be the judge of man's affairs. Man is material, of the earth. How long will you be ignorant of the reality of God? You are poisoned by the devil's touch. Why are you looking for a God that is not flesh and blood as you are? Spirits can only be found in another being like yourself. What pleasure would you have in an invisible world? And on the other hand what pleasure would spirits have in this material universe of ours? Your very nature is against your being anything other than a human being.

These are the days of the resurrection of the mentally dead so-called Negroes. The Son of Man is here. His coming has been fulfilled. He seeks that which was lost (the so called Negroes). Many now are receiving His name, and that name alone will save you. The wicked nations of the earth are sorry and angry to see the

Son of Man set up a government of justice and peace over this, their wicked world. They see signs in the heavens (sky) of great power to execute judgment on the world of the wicked, and they mourn.

We must have a new ruler and a new government, where the people can enjoy freedom, justice, and equality. Let the so-called Negroes rejoice for Allah has prepared for them what the eye has not seen, the ear has not heard, and the heart has not been able to conceive. The enemy knows this to be true and is now doing everything to prevent the so-called Negroes from seeing the hereafter. **Pgs. 18-19 MTBM**

Reference 104: Swine Forbidden

Deuteronomy 14:8
"The pig is also unclean; although it has a divided hoof, it does not chew the cud. You are not to eat their meat or touch their carcasses."

ON SPORT AND PLAY
(Chapter from MTBM By The Honorable Mr. Elijah Muhammad)

How can we say that we are the civilized people of the world when to be civilized, as Allah has taught me, one must have knowledge, wisdom, understanding, culture and refinement and not be savage. America, more than any other country, offers our people opportunities to engage in sports and play which cause delinquency, murder, theft and other forms of wicked and immoral crimes. This is due to this country's display of filthy temptations in this world of sport and play.

Great sums of money are spent in sport and play, in games of chance and gambling, in the operation of sporting houses. Millions are spent on horse racing and numbers rackets and are a disgraceful publicity of indecent sport.

Hundreds of millions of dollars change hands for the benefit of a few to the hurt of millions of poor people in the bread lines, and suffering from the lack of good education, with their last few pennies they help the already helped to try winning with these gambling "scientists" who have prepared a game of chance that the poor suckers have only one chance out of nine hundred to win. Therefore, the world of sports is causing tremendous evils.

Think over the destruction of homes and families, the disgrace, the shame, the filling up of jails -- state and federal -- with victims of sports and play, the loss of friendship, the loss of beautiful wives and husbands, the loss of sons and daughters to these penal institutions. From dope, knives and guns, this evil is practiced under Christianity.

The poor so-called Negroes are the worst victims in this world of sport and play because they are trying to learn the white man's games of civilization. Sport and play (games of chance) take away the remembrance of Allah (God) and the doing of good, says the Holy Qur-an. Think over what I am teaching, my people, and judge according to justice and righteousness.

Almighty Allah, to whom all praises are due, did not raise me as a Messenger like the Prophets of old, but he raised me as a Messenger, a Warner and a Reminder to the Nations of that which was prophesied to take place in these last days.

We have come to the end of the Prophets and the end of the old wicked world. I am missioned by the Supreme Being to awaken my people (so-called Negroes) to the time in which we are now living.

It is my people who are more ignorant to the truth than any other people on the planet earth. It is my people, furthermore, who are in the house of their enemies whom Allah is ready to destroy by fire. And they must be warned.

Finally, I must warn you against the devil's temptations, for they are seeking to make you unfit for acceptance into Allah's New World of peace, happiness and unlimited progress.

They have made you drunkards from their wine, whiskey and beer and other intoxicating. They have made prostitutes of our women. They have caused some of our women to love other women and men to love men and practice sex relations with their own sex. They have our people addicted to the worst kind of filth. They have made you dependent upon filth and vulgarity for survival.

They have made us eaters of the forbidden and poisoned swine. They have made us to have wicked, swearing mouths against the Most High God, Allah. But Allah knows the guilty ones, and you shall soon see the reality about which I have been warning you for the past 31 years made manifest in this rich, wicked world of Satan. Pgs. 246-247 MTBM

Reference 106: Ten Commandments

Exodus 20:1-18

This passage contains the Ten Commandments:
1. "I am the Lord your God, who brought you out of Egypt, out of the land of slavery. You shall have no other gods before me."

2. *"You shall not make for yourself an image in the form of anything in heaven above or on the earth beneath or in the waters below."*

3. *"You shall not misuse the name of the Lord your God, for the Lord will not hold anyone guiltless who misuses his name."*

4. *"Remember the Sabbath day by keeping it holy."*

5. *"Honor your father and your mother, so that you may live long in the land the Lord your God is giving you."*

6. *"You shall not murder."*

7. *"You shall not commit adultery."*

8. *"You shall not steal."*

9. *"You shall not give false testimony against your neighbor."*

10. *"You shall not covet your neighbor's house. You shall not covet your neighbor's wife, or his male or female servant, his ox or donkey, or anything that belongs to your neighbor."*

The enemy has tampered with the truth in both books: for he has been permitted to handle both books. Neither the Holy Qur-an nor the Bible was revealed with the intention of converting the white race into truth and righteousness; for God knew that there was no good in them the day they were created. But they are capable of deceiving you in regard to Allah and the righteous.

If you desire to preach or teach that a certain religion is true or right, you should know all religions and their scriptures. The man that God chooseth for Himself was among the people as a warner to them, such a one does not need previous training and knowledge, for Allah is his teacher and trainer.

The white man does not have knowledge of the Book that he is preaching.

The Bible's first five books (or Old Testament) are said to be Moses' Books. But it only mentions the giving of the Ten Commandments, and not a Book (Exodus 20:1-18).

I hope that you will not misunderstand me and think that I do not believe in Moses receiving the Torah. Nor does the New Testament open by saying: "This is a book or scripture revealed to Jesus," nor does Jesus tell us that He received a book. But yet the New Testament was revealed to Jesus, and the Revelation (the last Book of the Bible) was revealed to Yakub (titled John).

The Bible being tampered with by the Jews and the Christians has caused many divisions among the people because of their not understanding it. Since the creation of the white race, scripture after scripture along with many prophets have been given to the people of this world for the purpose of guiding and warning the righteous of their enemies, the devils. **Pg. 90 MTBM**

Reference 107: The Land Of Egypt

Exodus 16:2, 3, 8

Verse 2: "In the desert the whole community grumbled against Moses and Aaron."

Verse 3: "The Israelites said to them, 'If only we had died by the Lord's hand in Egypt! There we sat around pots of meat and ate all the food we wanted, but you have brought us out into this desert to starve this entire assembly to death.'"

Verse 8: "Moses also said, 'You will know that it was the Lord when he gives you meat to eat in the evening and all the bread you want in the morning, because he has heard your grumbling against him.'"

The Lord's Prayer, as it is called, contains some words that should not have been written there, such as: "Lead us not into temptation." God will not lead us into temptation. It is the devils that tempt us to sin. The above words show a lack of confidence in

God to lead us aright, that He must be reminded just how to lead us.

Another is: "Give us this day our daily bread." Here again, the words "this day" could lead one to believe that on that day the prayer was given, there was a shortage of bread, or that the Christians' prayers seek their physical bread first and spiritual bread last, even though the Bible says "You first seek the Kingdom of Heaven and all these things shall be added unto you." (Luke 12:31). In another place it says "Man shall not live by bread alone, but by every word that proceedeth out of the mouth of God" (Matthew 4:4).

These scriptures are contrary to the prayer, although it stands true of the Christians who seek bread, swine's flesh (the poison), whiskey, wine and beer first, and pray for spiritual food last.

The Bible shows (Exodus 16:2,3,8) that it was the want of bread and meat first of all that gave Moses and Aaron much trouble trying to lead the people into the spiritual knowledge of Jehovah and self-independence. They even said when they were hungry: "Would to God we had died by the hand of the Lord in the land of Egypt" (Exodus 16:3).

Ofttimes, they angered Moses and Aaron by their longing for the food of their slave-masters even while on their way to freedom and self-independence. **Pgs. 154-155 MTBM**

Reference 108: The Old Serpent Called Devil And Satan

Revelation 12:9

"The great dragon was hurled down—that ancient serpent called the devil, or Satan, who leads the whole world astray. He was hurled to the earth, and his angels with him."

That old serpent, called the devil and Satan, which deceiveth the whole world (Rev. 12:9) is a person or persons whose characteristics are like that of a serpent (snake). Serpents or snakes of the grafted type cannot be trusted, for they will strike you when you are not expecting a strike. **Pgs. 122-123 MTBM**

Reference 109: The Throne Of Iniquity

Psalms 94:20

"Can a corrupt throne be allied with you—a throne that brings on misery by its decrees?"

We have thousands of the darker people joining Islam all over the earth, but a very few whites accept Islam. The door of Islam has never been open to everyone who desired to accept it, but today it is different. The door of this religion is now being closed against the white race which has repeatedly rejected Islam, made mockery of it, persecuted and killed the Prophets and the believers (the followers), hid and concealed the truth of it and its God, Allah, who is the God of the Universe, and Islam, His only religion. They follow the poor teacher of Islam seeking a way or an excuse to kill him. They put spies (stool pigeons) on him to try to find a way to charge him with something other than the truth in order to do him evil for the truth's sake that he teaches.

As David says in his Psalms 94:20: "Shall the throne of iniquity have fellowship with thee, which frameth mischief by a law?" The poor lost-found members of the Tribe of Shabazz (nicknamed "Negroes" by their slavemasters) can well understand that they are the victims of such a frameup against them throughout America when they seek truth, love and unity among themselves. The white race does not want to see the poor black people of America united in Islam, a religion that is of Allah (God) backed by the spirit and power of God, to unite all of its believers into one nation of brotherhood. It is the only unifying religion known and tried by the races and nations of earth. This the white race knows. **Pg. 131 MTBM**

"How have these insights impacted you so far? Share your reflections and connect with like-minded believers in our private growing community. Your voice and perspective matter."

 https://nwnoicommunity.aitribes.app/ft/axkVr

Reference 110: Thee of Good and Evil

Genesis 2:17

"But you must not eat from the tree of the knowledge of good and evil, for when you eat from it you will certainly die."

The Bible's forbidden tree (Gen. 2:17) was a tree of the knowledge of good and evil. This also tells us that the tree was person, for trees know nothing! This tree of knowledge was forbidden to Adam and Eve. The only one whom this tree could be is the devil. After deceiving Adam and his wife, he has been called a serpent due to his keen knowledge of tricks and his acts of shrewdness; he made his acquaintance with Adam and his wife in the absence of God. Since this is the nature of a liar, he can best lie to the people when truth is absent.

Reference 101: They Love Their Master

Jeremiah 2:14

"Is Israel a servant, a slave by birth? Why then has he become plunder?"

FOR FREEDOM, JUSTICE, EQUALITY!
(Chapter from MTBM By The Honorable Mr. Elijah Muhammad)

With the fight going on in the South between the slaves and their masters, the slaves (in mind) have become home-born slaves as it is written (Jer. 2:14). They love their master and desire to be their master's kin in the line of true brotherhood. This is the truth which cannot be hidden in these modern times.

The intelligent people and the college university graduates are poisoned 100 per cent more in mind and into the love of the enemy than the uneducated. It is no wonder that the scriptures say the poor gladly receive the truth as being offered heaven at once from Almighty Allah (God) Himself.

According to black men's actions and rejection of Allah and the true religion, Islam, which means entire submission to the will of Allah, they will take all kinds of humiliation. They are beaten and killed by the white man (the real citizen and owner of the land) while trying to force him to admit them (the once slaves) as equals to the white race.

I have taught for years that you cannot demand the white man accept you as his equal or as his brother, because he is intelligent enough to know that you are not his equal and that you are not his brother. Even if you go back to Adam -- he is not the black man's father. We are not all compatible. Adam is the father of the white man. This is known.

The suffering of my people in trying to force themselves on the white man in the South and elsewhere as their brothers and sisters is to be pitied. I, for one, have true love for them, and I pity them. But I cannot help them when they deliberately walk away from God. By their deeds and acts they indicate they would rather help the enemy, the murderer and those who hate them than help God Almighty, Whose proper name is Allah and who came in the person of Master Fard Muhammad and to whom praises are due forever.

The best and most intelligent way is to give Caesar what is Caesar's and let us go for ourselves on some of this earth that we can call our own, just as did the white people. When Europe was overpopulated, they found expansion in the Western Hemisphere.

If we want freedom, justice and equality, we must look for it among ourselves and our kind, not among the people who have destroyed and robbed us of even the knowledge of ourselves, themselves, our God and our religion.

We have a world of Muslims under Allah and His religion, Islam. The white people do not teach you this because it points the way to your freedom and equality. It is a shame that our people are beaten and killed because of their ignorance in wanting to be white people, while there are billions of people on the face of this earth who look like them but only 400 million white people on our planet earth.

Our population runs into billions, and the earth belongs to us. We are the original owners of the earth and will take it and rule it again. This is the time. **Pgs. 232-233 MTBM MTBM**

Reference 112: Thou Forsaken Me

Matthew 27:46

"About three in the afternoon Jesus cried out in a loud voice, 'Eli, Eli, lema sabachthani?' (which means 'My God, my God, why have you forsaken me?')"

It is foolish to believe in three gods-foolish to make Jesus the Son and the equal of His Father (the one of 2,000 years ago). If Jesus said in His suffering "My God, My God, why hast Thou forsaken Me?" (Matthew 27:46) then most surely He did not recognize Himself as being the equal of God, and no other scripture shows Jesus as the equal of God. **Pg. 27 MTBM**

Reference 115: To Be Destroyed

Revelation 19:20

"But the beast was captured, and with it the false prophet who had performed the signs on its behalf. With these signs he had deluded those who had received the mark of the beast and worshiped its image. The two of them were thrown alive into the fiery lake of burning sulfur."

Daniel 7:11, 19

Verse 11: "Then I continued to watch because of the boastful words the horn was speaking. I kept looking until the beast was slain and its body destroyed and thrown into the blazing fire."

Verse 19: "Then I wanted to know the meaning of the fourth beast, which was different from all the others and most terrifying, with its iron teeth and bronze claws—the beast that crushed and devoured its victims and trampled underfoot whatever was left."

The black people, and especially the so-called Negroes, are now in the very area where God has said to me that the fire (often referred to as the "fire of hell" or "hell fire") will begin which will destroy the present wicked white race of America first. The sins of the white race are far worse and more pungent to the nostril of God than the sins of Sodom and Gomorrah! The fire of hell is not intended for the so-called Negroes: only those who, after hearing this teaching of the truth which I am giving to you and the warnings of Allah (God), will wilfully hold on to the white race and their religion, Christianity.

The so-called Negroes are made so poisoned by this wicked race of devils that they love them more than they love their own people. It is really because of the evil done to them by the American white race that Allah (God) has put them on His list, as the first to be destroyed. The others will be given a little longer to live, as the prophet Daniel says (7:11, 19 and Rev. 19:20). Believe it, or let it alone, the above refers to America. She is the only white government out of the European race that answers the description of the symbolic Fourth Beast. The so-called Negroes are warned to come out of her (America) (Rev. 18:4), though the truth of Daniel and Revelations could not be told until the time of the end of this prophecy.

The Bible means good if you can rightly understand it. My interpretation of it is given to me from the Lord of the Worlds. Yours is your own and from the enemies of the truth. The so-called Negroes will be the lucky ones, that is, if they stop following and practicing the evils and indecent doings of this wicked and doomed race of devils (whose true self has been a secret for 6,000 years).

So-called Negroes, accept your own God, religion and people so that you may be successful in escaping the fire! **Pg. 88 MTBM**

Reference 116: Truth Make You Free

John 8:32

"Then you will know the truth, and the truth will set you free."

It is against the very nature of God and man, and other life, to love their enemies. Would God ask us to do that which He, Himself, can't do? He hates his enemies so much that He tells us that He is going to destroy them in hell fire, along with those of us who follow His enemies.

The misunderstanding of the Old and New Testaments by the so-called Negro preachers makes it our graveyard and must be resurrected therefrom. Moses didn't teach a resurrection of the dead nor did Noah, who was a prophet before Moses. The New Testament and Holy Qur-an's teaching of a resurrection of the dead can't mean the people who have died physically and returned to the earth, but rather a mental resurrection of us, the black nation, who are mentally dead to the knowledge of truth; the truth of self, God and the arch-enemy of God and His people.

That is that Truth (John 8:32) that will make us free, whereof John (8:32) doesn't say what truth shall make you free; therefore leaving it questionable and to the advantage of the enemy. Oh, that my poor people, the so-called Negroes could understand, they would sit in heaven at once. The enemy is alert, wide-awake and even on the job to prevent the so-called Negroes from believing Allah and the true religion of Allah (God) and His

Prophets, the Religion of Islam. The enemy is well aware that Allah (God) is the Rock of our Defense and Islam the House of our Salvation. Woe to you who try to hinder the teachings of Islam and the truth of God and the devil, also ever planning the death of the Messenger of Allah and his followers. It would have been better that you were not born. The chastisement of Allah shall abide upon you until you are brought to shame and disgrace.

Remember the disgrace suffered by Pharaoh and his people for their opposition to Moses and his followers, just because Pharaoh feared that Moses would teach this people the true religion, Islam! Pharaoh set his whole army against Moses only to be brought to naught. Pharaoh had deceived his slaves in the knowledge of Allah and the true religion Islam, and indirectly had them worshiping him and his people as God.

The poor so-called Negroes are so filled with fear of their enemy that they stoop to helping the enemy, against their own salvation. Be aware of what you are doing lest you be the worst loser. If they had only been taught the truth, they would act differently. The Bible, church and Christianity have deceived them. I pray Allah to give them life and light of understanding.
Pgs. 96-97 MTBM

Reference 117: Under Name Of Israel

2 Chronicles 6:31-39

This passage contains Solomon's prayer of dedication, where he asks for God's forgiveness and protection for Israel if they sin and repent.

2 Chronicles 6:31

"so that they will fear you and walk in obedience to you all the time they live in the land you gave our ancestors."

2 Chronicles 6:32

"As for the foreigner who does not belong to your people Israel but has come from a distant land because of your great name and your mighty hand and your outstretched arm—when they come and pray toward this temple,"

2 Chronicles 6:33

"then hear from heaven, your dwelling place. Do whatever the foreigner asks of you, so that all the peoples of the earth may know your name and fear you, as do your own people Israel, and may know that this house I have built bears your Name."

2 Chronicles 6:34

"When your people go to war against their enemies, wherever you send them, and when they pray to you toward this city you have chosen and the temple I have built for your Name,"

2 Chronicles 6:35

"then hear from heaven their prayer and their plea, and uphold their cause."

2 Chronicles 6:36

"When they sin against you—for there is no one who does not sin—and you become angry with them and give them over to the enemy, who takes them captive to a land far away or near;"

2 Chronicles 6:37

"and if they have a change of heart in the land where they are held captive, and repent and plead with you in the land of their captivity and say, 'We have sinned, we have done wrong and acted wickedly';"

==2 Chronicles 6:38==

"and if they turn back to you with all their heart and soul in the land of their captivity where they were taken, and pray toward the land you gave their ancestors, toward the city you have chosen and toward the temple I have built for your Name;"

==2 Chronicles 6:39==

"then from heaven, your dwelling place, hear their prayer and their pleas, and uphold their cause. And forgive your people, who have sinned against you."

It is a prayer for forgiveness that Solomon advised you and me to make to Allah if we be lost from our own under the name of Israel (II Chronicles 6:36-39). Solomon was a Muslim prophet and king. He and his father David, were of the black nation. He advised us to pray toward our own land and toward the Holy City (Mecca) which He has chosen.

In the parables of the prodigal son (which is one of the most beautiful) and of the lost sheep it is, or should be, easier for the so-called Negroes to see that they are the ones referred to. It is with the turning toward his home and father's house to pray that the sins of the prodigal son were forgiven, and he was accepted by his father and restored to his rightful place among his brethren. It is the turning again of the lost-found so-called Negro – the tribe of Shabazz -- in prayer to Allah, their true God and His true religion, Islam, that they will be seated in heaven overnight (at once). The enemy knows this as well as I. **Pg.138 MTBM**

Reference 118: Weapons No Good Against Allah

Revelation 16:6

"For they have shed the blood of your holy people and your prophets, and you have given them blood to drink as they deserve."

The slave-masters' every cry is to beat- beat- kill- kill- the so-called Negroes. Maybe the day has arrived that Allah will return to the devils -- that which they have been so anxious to pour on the poor innocent so-called Negroes. Allah will give you your own blood to drink like water and your arms and allies will not help you against him (Rev. 16:6).

The heads and bodies of the so-called Negroes are used to test the clubs and guns of the devils, and yet the poor, foolish, so-called Negroes admire the devils regardless to how they are treated.

America is now under Divine Plagues. One will come after the other until she is destroyed. Allah has said it. **Pgs. 128-129 MTBM**

Reference 119: Who Is Able To Make War

Daniel 7:7

"After that, in my vision at night I looked, and there before me was a fourth beast—terrifying and frightening and very powerful. It had large iron teeth; it crushed and devoured its victims and trampled underfoot whatever was left. It was different from all the former beasts, and it had ten horns."

Reference 120: Who Is Like Unto The Beast

Revelation 13:4
"People worshiped the dragon because he had given authority to the beast, and they also worshiped the beast and asked, 'Who is like the beast? Who can wage war against it?'"

THE BEAST PART I
(Chapter from MTBM By The Honorable Mr. Elijah Muhammad)

Who is like unto the beast? Who is able to make war with him? (Rev. 13:4). This beast that is spoken of in the prophecy of the first book of the Bible called Revelations and has and still is being much misunderstood by my people. But one thing is certain, the name (beast) is believed by most all readers of the Book to refer to a person or persons, which is right. But who is the person or persons? (Note: There is mentioned in the same chapter and verse a dragon which gave power to the beast. Who can this dragon be? Is he also a person? Then how are the two related?)

The eighteenth verse of the same chapter reads: Here is wisdom. Let him that hath understanding count the number of the beast: for it is the number of a man. Here we are told that the number of the beast referred to here is a man or people. Now the only way of knowing just what man or people is to watch and see what man or people's doings or works compare with the doings and works of the symbolic beast of the Revelation.

This name beast, when given to a person, refers to that person's characteristics, not to an actual beast. Study the history of how America treats the freedom, justice and equality which is supposed to be given to all citizens of America (of course, the

Negroes are not citizens of America). A citizen cannot and will not allow his people and government to treat him in such way as America treats her so-called Negroes.

To call a person a beast is simply to say, according to the English language: Nouns -- violent person, berserk or berserker, demon, fiend, shaitan or sheitan or Satan, or dragon, evil spirit, Satanas, devil, diable, Iblis, azazel, abaddon, apollyon, the prince of the devils, the prince of darkness, the prince of this world, the prince of the power of air, the wicked one, the evil one, the archenemy, the archfied, the devil incarnate, the father of lies, the author and father of evil, the serpent, the common enemy, the angel of the bottomless pit. Adjectives -- satanic, devilish, diabolic (al), hell-born, demoniac, savage, brute, fierce, vicious, wild, untamed, tameless, ungentle, barbarous, unmitigated, unsoftened, ungovernable, uncontrollable (obstinate), brute force, forcibly, by main, with might and main, by force of arms, at the point of the sword or bayonet (the devil and Satan). The above in the explanation of beast when applied to human beings or people in general, according to Roget's International Thesaurus. The so-called American Negroes have and still suffer under such brutish treatment from the American Christian white race, who call themselves followers of Jesus and his God.

The Revelator could not have better described the white race's way of dealing with the black nation. They (white race) are the people described as beast in the Revelation of the Bible. Study them and their history and dealings with people and you will without hesitation agree with me 100 per cent that these are the people meant by the Revelator who foresaw their future and end and wrote it while he and his followers were in exile from the Holy Land 6,600 years ago on the Island of Pelan in the Aegean Sea, where he grafted the present white race.

The revelation is claimed by the Christians to have been grafted to a Saint John Divine who was a follower of Jesus, but this is erroneous and wrong. It is by the father of the white race (Mr. Yakub or Jacob). The people other than the beast are mentioned as worshipers of the beast: And they (the people of the darker nation) worshipped the dragon which gave power unto the beast. The power given by the dragon to the beast refers to a higher wisdom and knowledge of the time and wise preparedness. The chief head and spiritual guidance of the white race is the Pope of Rome. **Pgs. 124-126 MTBM**

"The journey to understanding is not meant to be traveled alone. Our community welcomes those who seek knowledge and are ready to engage in meaningful discussions about these teachings. Join us and connect with others who are committed to the truth."

 https://nwnoicommunity.aitribes.app/ft/axkVr

Reference 121: Wicked Watches The Righteous

Psalms 37:32

"The wicked lie in wait for the righteous, intent on putting them to death."

It stands true that they are enemies of the truth by their ever warring against the truth. They know that Islam is the truth; they know that the history of them that God has revealed to me is the truth but do not like for you to know such truth of them. Therefore, they seek every means to oppose this teaching. They try everyone of you that say that you believe it and are my followers. They are watching you and me, seeking a chance to do us harm. They are so upset and afraid that they visit you at your homes to question you of your sincerity of Islam.

As David said in his Psalms (37:32): "The wicked watcheth the righteous and seeketh to stay him". Also, Psalms (37:30): "The mouth of the righteous speaketh wisdom, and his tongue talketh of judgment." And in another place (Psa. 94:16): "Who will rise up for me against the workers of iniquity?" I have answered Him and said, "Here I am, take me." For the evil done against my people (the so-called Negroes) I will not keep silent until He executes judgment and defends my cause. Fear not my life, for He is well able to defend it. Know that God is a man and not a spook! Pg. 10 MTBM

Reference 123: Worship White Man As God

Revelation 14:4

"These are those who did not defile themselves with women, for they remained virgins. They follow the Lamb wherever he goes. They were purchased from among mankind and offered as firstfruits to God and the Lamb."

VICTORY OF THE APOSTLE
(Chapter from MTBM By The Honorable Mr. Elijah Muhammad)

THE HYPOCRITES *'Announce to the hypocrites that they shall have a painful chastisement. 'Allah will gather together the hypocrites and the unbelievers all in hell. 'Surely the hypocrites strive to deceive Allah, and He shall requite their deceit to them. 'Surely the hypocrites are in the lowest stage of the fire and you shall not find a helper for them except those who repent and amend* *and hold fast to Allah and are sincere in the obedience to Allah. These are with believers and Allah will grant the believers a mighty reward" (Holy Qur-an 4:140, 142, 145 and 138).*

The Holy Qur-an has the same announcement for all disbelievers and hypocrites of the Messenger. It is also the same given to Noah and his followers. It is the same given to all disbelieving foes and hypocrites. The hypocrites around Moses, Jesus and Muhammad were given the same warnings. And, they (the hypocrites) are prophesied in the Holy Qur-an (which is a very true book), to be the same type of hypocrites and to be saying the same word to the last Apostle and his true followers today as they did to the former prophets and their followers.

My followers here in America -- and the hypocrites among them -- are now being manifested to be the same as all others in the past. They hypocrites utter the same words, make mockery of the Messenger and his followers, and plan to do harm to us just as the hypocrites of the past did all other Messengers and their followers.

The Holy Qur-an says to the last Apostle: "All Apostles before you were mocked and called liars, but Allah reminds the last Apostle to think of His disapproval of other hypocrites and disbelievers."

He destroyed them and some of the hypocrites returned after they had tasted of the chastisement. We have, today, such a perfect fulfillment of the prophecy of the Qur-an in the recent outbreak of hypocrisy among my followers. The chief hypocrite of them all -- and the worst of them all -- has never stopped in his attempt to do harm to my mission.

The Holy Qur-an teaches: they will fight you with their tongues and even with their hands. So their tongues were not sufficient; they wanted quick action. So, the chief hypocrite resorted to arming his followers, as well as himself, with .30 caliber weapons. Knowing that my followers and I had not resorted to such weapons, they intended to spring a surprise attack by mowing us down. What happened? He and his ignorant followers had forgotten that God was with me and my followers. They did not know they could not stop us with weapons. The hypocrites always will be the losers.

This chief hypocrite took a group with him to build a "Mosque in opposition" to me and filled it with all types of wickedness and disbelievers like himself. He wished the praise of the people and not of God. He has said everything imaginable against me, which likely will hurt him and those who follow him more than he thinks. He wants the world to recognize him as a qualified leader. He should seek the recognition of Allah. Allah is the One who makes a leader for his people.

This chief hypocrite is not with Allah; if he were with Allah, he would be with me. Since he is not with Allah, he cannot claim guidance from Allah. He has admitted that he cannot trust a religion and cannot trust a God who teaches when to act. He wants to act when he is ready to act, rather than depend upon a God who will act in His own good time.

He does not wait on a God like that. Many other such fools passed away in great dishonor and shame long before this chief hypocrite. No weapons (as it is written) formed against me will prosper as long as Allah is with me and I am with Allah, because the twain will never break. We always shall be together against the enemy and together for the believers. Some of the hypocrites have come to know all of these things, but they must be punished.

A hypocrite is one who first says he believes in Islam and then disbelieves and seeks to oppose the Messenger and those who believe in him and his God. Their punishment -- says the Holy Qur-an in several places -- is grief, regret, shame and disgrace. I will never forget this hypocrite's hateful acts against me.

If he is the last of the 22 million, I shall remind him of his evil and wicked acts done to me in return for the good that I did for him. He could not have risen up against me if I had not given him so much knowledge of Allah and his religion. When I made him a leader and a teacher among the people, he felt proud. He now thinks that he should be elected top man, but I am sure that he will be appointed the lowest man.

He went, first, on the side of the Muslims, and then on the side of the devils, and again on the side of the Muslims and against the devils. He is -- as the Holy Qur-an says -- neither this nor that. His greatest desire is for someone to declare him as their leader. He is insane for leadership and disgraces himself for that office. As I have repeatedly taught -- and the scholars and scientists will agree with me -- the so-called Negro must have divine leadership today. The leader must be divinely appointed, not self-made or made by the people. This is universally known; I am that man, divinely appointed by Allah.

According to the Bible and Holy Qur-an, punishment is sure to overtake hypocrites and those who seek to oppose Allah and His Apostle. I quote here a verse from the Holy Qur-an.

"Do they not know that whoever acts in opposition to Allah and His Apostle, he shall surely have the fire of hell to abide in it, that is the grievous abasement" (Holy Qur-an 9:63).

That is the hell that the hypocrites and disbelievers will suffer, and it begins with their feeling of fear and excitement -- fear that someone is going to do harm to them (as they plan to harm those they oppose). There is no fear for a true believer, nor shall he grieve. This grief of the hypocrties, according to the Holy Qur-an, prostrates them and makes them wish that they were dead. They even wish for someone to kill them.

But Allah, the Holy Qur-an says, will not permit anyone to kill them, because death would take them out of their chastisement and grief. They will not bow in submission to the will of Allah and obedience in following His Messenger, and after a year or so under this condition, they are classified with the devil, to be destroyed in hellfire -- the final end to both.

The Bible's last book, under the title of Revelation of John, prophesies a grief falling upon the followers (the so-called American Negro) of the symbolic beast (the white man) who are in the beast's names and who worship and believe in the white man's religion, called Christianity. They worship the white man as though he were god above the Supreme God of heaven and earth. They also worship the white man's leader of the Christian religion, the Pope in Rome. This is mentioned in Revelation 14:4.

The grief of the hypocrites is such that even the victim is not able to say his prayers. In the first place, God has closed the door and does not hear the prayers of the hypocrites when He sends chastisement upon them. This is in store for my hypocrites and shall befall them at any time -- just as it did the hypocrites of 1935. We actually witnessed this type of chastisement that fell upon those hypocrites in 1935. One of the hypocrites then was my own brother, and another was a minister by the name of Augustus Muhammad, my top assistant at that time in the Chicago Mosque No. 2. They felt proud after they had acquired a little wisdom and thought that they were more powerful than the teacher.

I have been told directly by some of the hypocrites that they think it is time for a change and that a younger man should take my place. And they even go so far as to designate a person whom they think should take my place.

I look at them and say within myself, "What a fool you are! How can you appoint someone to take my place when I did not appoint myself? God, Almighty appointed me. You are foolish to play with God's mission and His messenger to the mentally dead nation. You take it lightly that you can vote out, put down or shoot down God's Messenger and set up another of your choice. What will you do with the next group of hypocrites who may not like the man of your choice? They may shoot both you and your man down and take over."

Let the hypocrites be aware that there is a great chastisement in store for them -- and their aims, purposes and wishes will never materialize. The Holy Qur-an teaches that their grief will be so severe that it will prostrate them and they will be unable even to blink their eyes -- and that which they feared will come to pass. What they actually feared is:

Exposure as the losers who had lied. Punishment for wishing their grief upon the Messenger and those with him. Victory of the Messenger over them.

They shall suffer the loss of true friendship, and they are not helped. They go to the devil for friendship, and he turns them down because he knows that they will not be able to help him against Allah and the Apostle, because Allah and His Apostle are considered submerged into one.

The Apostle is considered one in Allah and Allah is one in the Apostle. So, when you look at one, you see both; when you hear one speak, you hear both, because they both are as one in their agreement for the right and against the disbeliever. Therefore,

Allah brings this to pass. As it was in Noah's day, so shall it be in the day of the last Apostle, whom God raises from the mentally dead Negroes in North America. **Pgs. 26-0264 MTBM**

Reference 124: Ye Have Condemned And Killed The Just

James 5:6

"You have condemned and murdered the innocent one, who was not opposing you."

The government only wants to pacify her once slaves with fancy false promises that she knows she cannot fulfill without the loss of friendship and bloodshed among her own people. But there is nothing like a good future in these rosy promises for the so-called Negroes. Why should the government hinder us?

We want some of this earth and its treasures of raw materials to build us an independent nation as you and other nations have done. We want to live in peace. It is impossible to get along with you in peace while you cannot even get along with each other in peace! We were created of the essence of peace, while you were created of the essence of evilness, and evilness you will always do to either self or others.

That awful day of yours will surely come -- the appointed hour you are hasting by your evil intentions and doings to us, the poor black people. We who have given our sweat and blood all our lives today we cry for justice, and you send your armed forces with trained wild dogs to kill us as it is written of you. "Ye have condemned and killed the just, and he doth not resist you" (James 5:6).

You send armies of heavily armed policemen to slay the unarmed so-called Negroes. Does this act of murder of unarmed people show that you are brave or cowards? You, like your fathers, hate and despise your slaves, and you beat and murder them daily. And after such inhuman treatment you want them to love you so that you may carry out your evil doings on them without resistance.

The beating and killing of those among us who say they are Muslims is most surely hasting your doom. You hate them because Allah has revealed the truth of you to them and you are angry and seek to take revenge on them for what Allah has made known to them of truth. **Pg. 258 MTBM**

Reference 114: You Should Not Have Fellowship With Devils

1 Corinthians 10:21
"You cannot drink the cup of the Lord and the cup of demons too; you cannot have a part in both the Lord's table and the table of demons."

A NATION WITHIN A NATION

From a few comes a great nation. The Lord God of Islam taught me that in 1555 a devil by the name of John Hawkins, or Hopkins, of England brought the first of our parents here for slave purposes. We were not to be citizens, not to be represented as human or to be given equal justice under the American laws.

In 300 years of slavery, we were lashed, beaten and killed; given no education; and reared and cared for like the slave-master's stock (horses, cows and other domestic animals). Our children were separated to different plantation owners. For the last approximately 100 years of so-called freedom, the so-called Negroes have been subjected to the worst inhuman treatment of any people who have ever lived on the earth. They (the devils) have lynched and burned the so-called Negroes during the past century as sport for their wives and children to enjoy!

Edwin R. Embree states in his book, "Brown Americans," page 169, that "the burning of Henry Lowry in Arkansas, proceeded by inches. Leaves soaked in gasoline were heaped about in small bundles so that torture would be dragged out. Ralph Roddy, a reporter, described the entire orgy in the Memphis press of January 27, 1921. He was able to cover the story because plans for the lynching had been made well in advance. The newspapers were notified to be ready to issue extras. When Henry Smith was burned at the stake in Texas, excursion trains were run for the event. Many women and children were in the throng that gloated over the suffering of the victim." This is something the teachers and leaders of the so-called Negroes should teach their children -- the evil and murder of their people by these blue-eyed white devils. Instead, because of their fear of the white blue-eyed devils, the so-called Negro parents teach their children just the opposite. Their doctrine is "love your enemies" and "do not hate those who mistreat you." That is, if it is a white person! But if he is a Negro, kill or beat the hell out of him!

The so-called Negro leaders know the white devils do not care about a Negro killing another Negro. 5 How can we keep our younger people of the present day from loving their open enemies, the devils? The Lord, God of Righteousness, dislikes any one of us who loves these white blue-eyed devils. He threatens to send every one of us to hell with the devils who show love for them, love to be called by the devil's names or worship their images. Read your Bible and Holy Qur-an.

Edwin Embree, also on the same page, mentions what Walter White, deceased secretary of NAACP, said he heard and saw in Florida. In his book, "Rope and Faggot," White recounts the gruesome tale of lynching in this country. While investigating an atrocious riot in Florida, White was met, he says, by three clean healthy children (white) headed for school. None were over 9 years of age. They gleefully described the event and "the fun we had burning the niggers."

Do thank Allah for revealing this evil deceitful open enemy, "the devil!" The devil has deceived most of the world of black people. They have nearly nine-tenths of the black people headed to their doom with them. Curse be to the black man or woman who loves this open enemy, the devil, and hates his own black skin and kind! May the chastisement of Allah choke you until you submit that: Thee is no God but Allah and that Muhammad in the wilderness of North America is His Messenger! After all of this evil we have suffered at the very hands of these devils, we have become a Nation in a Nation. We must now be separated from them and given a place on this earth that we can call our own!

They, the white race, cannot treat you and me with justice and equality. They cannot do so among themselves. Even though they are against us. This does not mean that they have love and peace for each other. No! They war against each other all the time. They are devils. No heart of love and mercy are in them as you may think. Nature did not give them such a heart.

The Bible warns us against the love and worship of these devils. Psalms 106:37, says "Yea, they sacrificed their sons and their daughters unto devils." In another place it states, "And I would not that you should have fellowship with devils. Ye cannot drink the cup of the Lord, and the cup of the devils: ye cannot be partakers of the Lord's table and of the table of the devils. (1 Cor. 10:-21). "They should not worship up devils" (Rev. 9:20).

The so-called Negroes, because of their fear and ignorance of this real open enemy devil, will fall victim to them if we do not constantly warn them of the consequences.

I am willing to die for the so-called Negro that they may see and understand the truth of self, God and this race of devils.

We have served them well through ignorance and blindness because of being without a teacher. Allah (God) has given you one. I, Elijah Muhammad am from God, Himself! Why not believe and follow me? Are you afraid of being persecuted for the sake of truth to this 22 million blind, deaf and dumb lost-found Nation of Islam? In that case, your life is already doomed. **Pgs. 230-232 MTBM**

"The path to deeper understanding does not stop here. For those seeking further knowledge, the 'Pillars of Knowledge' Bundle offers essential teachings to strengthen your foundation and expand your wisdom."

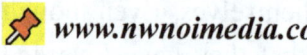 www.nwnoimedia.com

"Knowledge is a responsibility. The mission continues, and your support helps keep this truth alive. If you have found value in these teachings, consider contributing to ensure that others receive the same guidance."

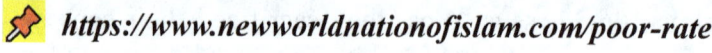 https://www.newworldnationofislam.com/poor-rate

NWNOI PUBLICATIONS

The Future Master Fard Muhammad
ISBN:978-0-9890425-0-5
Publication Date: 2/1/2013
Avaliable Now $12.95
Send Orders to:
NWNOI Publications
PO Box 8466
Newark, NJ 07108

Knowledge of The Gods
ISBN:978-0-9890425-2-9
Publication Date: 4/28/2015
Avaliable Now $16.99
Send Orders to:
NWNOI Publications
PO Box 8466
Newark, NJ 07108

AL-Fard: The Dawn
ISBN:978-1-947732-17-9
Publication Date: 4/10/2018
Avaliable Now $16.99

Send Orders to:
NWNOI Publications
PO Box 8466
Newark, NJ 07108

S/H $4.25 for 1 book, $6.25 for 2 books, $9.25 for 3 books

www.ingramcontent.com/pod-product-compliance
Lightning Source LLC
Chambersburg PA
CBHW050248010526
44107CB00003B/237